SKETCHES FROM LIFE

Books by
DEAN ACHESON

Sketches from Life
Power and Diplomacy
A Citizen Looks at Congress
A Democrat Looks at His Party

SKETCHES FROM LIFE
Of Men I Have Known
DEAN ACHESON

HARPER & BROTHERS, NEW YORK

To A.S.A.
Sharer of the Burden
and
Heroine of These Events

CONTENTS

Introduction   *xiii*

I   ERNEST BEVIN   *1*

II   ROBERT SCHUMAN   *31*

III WINSTON SPENCER CHURCHILL   *61*

IV   A RUSSIAN GALLERY   *85*

V   LISBON: BACKGROUND OF A
     CONFERENCE   *107*

VI   ARTHUR VANDENBERG AND
     THE SENATE   *123*

VII GENERAL MARSHALL   *147*

VIII KONRAD ADENAUER   *167*

IX   A STATE VISIT: VIENNA, 1952   *181*
     Afterword   *199*
     Index   *201*

Eight pages of photographs will be found following page 64.

I wish to acknowledge with gratitude
permission generously given me to use in these *Sketches*
material which has previously appeared in the
American Heritage about Senator Vandenberg and
in *The Reporter* about General Marshall.

D. A.

INTRODUCTION

To many people "diplomacy" means one of two things. To some it is a fussy life of social or official minuet—"the sort of steady-going diplomacy," writes Ann Bridge in *Peking Picnic,* "which enables a Minister to say in almost every dispatch, 'I repeated to His Excellency what I had said to him last week,' or vice versa." To others, diplomacy is dreadfully solemn and serious, made up of missions to Moscow, Geneva, or the United Nations to save the world from nuclear disaster, or to present our shining "image" to a doubting world. In truth, it has something of both, but happily something else besides. Like all of life, it has its humorous interludes, sometimes comic, even ridiculous ones. These are in payment for much dullness and hard work. The wise laborer in the diplomatic vineyard will receive them with joy and cherish them in his heart against the evil hours when no man may smile.

For me there has been another payment, too—the opportunity to work with and to know some remarkable men. With some of them I formed deep and lasting friendships. All of them enriched my experience. By these sketches I hope that the reader may see them as living people, not as mere names or symbols standing for what we may like or dislike. Lord Chesterfield, who was no fool, wrote to his son, "You must look into people, as well as at them." As over some years I looked into the men depicted here, I saw, not official figures with titles standing for policies which my government approved or disapproved, but individuals with very human qualities. For the most part I liked the possessors of these qualities. To some of them I became devoted.

As I think of them, they seem most alive in the lighter and gayer moments which relieved our work; and more than relieved it; indeed, did much to bring to fruition some of the results of these productive years. For, while these sketches by no means aspire to the heights of diplomatic history, they cover the period, from the end of the Second World War to the beginning of 1953, in which American foreign policy was remade to cope with a wholly new world—the years of the rescue of Greece, Turkey, and the Eastern Mediterranean; of the Marshall Plan; of NATO; and of the meeting of the armed assault on South Korea. These events are mentioned only to remind the reader that behind the personal relationships and the light moments recalled here was a somber background.

SKETCHES FROM LIFE

I

ERNEST BEVIN

British Secretary of State for
Foreign Affairs, 1945–1951

Before I met Ernest Bevin, two Secretaries of State I had
served gave me differing impressions of him. Neither prepared me for his quality. Mr. Byrnes liked him; General
Marshall did not. In the General's case, the trouble came,
I later felt sure, from a misunderstanding. In December,
1947, it became clear that Molotov was stalling the Conference of Foreign Ministers being held in London. The three
Western Ministers agreed that at the beginning of the next
session General Marshall would blast Molotov, and then,
upon Bevin's motion, they would immediately adjourn the
conference. The General fired the blast, but Bevin made
no motion. So, after some confusion, the General had to
make it. He felt that he had been let down and that Bevin
was not reliable, a black mark in the General's scale of
judgments.

After I came to know Bevin well, what had happened was
as clear as day to me. Bevin was no split-second operator. He
moved slowly; he was often distracted. He could easily miss
a cue and in the resulting confusion not know how to pick
it up again. To a soldier, trained to precision in maneuver,
what was really clumsiness appeared deliberate. This was a
misjudgment. Ernest Bevin was as honorable and loyal a
colleague as one could wish.

But Bevin admired General Marshall. To him the Marshall Plan was—and rightly so—one of history's greatest acts
of statesmanship. He told me that, as he finished reading the
General's speech at Harvard in June, 1947, Sir William (now
Lord) Strang, Permanent Under Secretary of State for Foreign
Affairs, came to him with the suggestion that he should in-
struct the Washington Embassy to inquire at the State Department what General Marshall meant by his speech.

"Bill," he said, "we know what he *said*. If you ask questions, you'll get answers you don't want. Our problem is
what *we do,* not what *he meant.*" And he began to act at
once to establish the Paris conference on European recovery.

We met first in the spring of 1949, when the signing of the
North Atlantic Treaty furnished an opportunity for personal consultation and concurrence with the British and
French Foreign Ministers on two matters of first importance.
One was too secret for cable communication, which involved
too many people; the other, too complicated. The first was
the discussion with Stalin, then nearing a conclusion, about
ending the blockade of Berlin; the other, the creation of a
federal German government by uniting the three Western
Zones of Occupation. The Kremlin had been trying without
success to make the former contingent upon our abandoning
the latter.

Bevin and the French Foreign Minister, Robert Schuman,
at our invitation, came to Washington a few days before the
larger gathering. Never were two men more unlike, or more
congenial to work with. Bevin, short and too fat, suffered
cruelly from attacks of angina, but continued to eat heartily
and drink his whiskey sodas. His gait was the rolling one of
a fat man; his clothes gave the impression of being enormous.
His best feature was his eyes which, even behind heavy,
horn-rimmed spectacles, lit up a face made undistinguished

by an unusually broad and flat nose above full lips.

Anything was likely to happen with Ernie Bevin, and usually did. A quick temper could flash without warning, and often seemingly by accident, but was defenseless against good humor. He did not bear grudges, was not sensitive in the sense of being touchy. He worked hard, understood the full significance of the Soviet aggressive policy of 1946, and respected and used the Foreign Office staff, which in turn adored him. One of the satisfactions of working with him was the knowledge that his standing with the Prime Minister, the British public, and the Trades Union Congress was such that what Bevin said could be taken as British foreign policy.

Bevin was something new in the Foreign Office. He could hardly have been more different from his two immediate predecessors, Mr. Anthony Eden and the Earl of Halifax. Born in a remote village in West England on the edge of the Exmoor Forest, son of a domestic servant and an unknown father, he was left an orphan at the age of eight, and left school at eleven. But his education by no means ended then.* Forever learning, forever reading and studying, in Baptist chapel and trade union study groups, in the Bristol Socialist Society, he sought books and debate wherever they were available. His Odyssey saw him bakeshop boy at sixpence a week, van boy, waiter, horse-tram conductor, lunchroom operator, until he came to temporary rest as teamster for a mineral-water company. His dray took him into every street and alley in Bristol, where the poverty and misery of the working people and the ignorant indifference of the society around them were burned upon his heart and mind. All this burst out in the peroration of one of his greatest speeches:

* Mr. Alan Bullock's *The Life and Times of Ernest Bevin* (Heinemann, London, 1960), Vol. 1, is my source of information on Bevin's early life. This truly great book is more than a biography. It is a history of the working people of England and their labor movement from 1880 to 1940.

> If your Court refuse our claim . . . go to the
> Prime Minister . . . tell him to close our schools,
> tell him that industry can only be run by artisan
> labour on the pure fodder or animal basis, teach us
> nothing, let us learn nothing. . . . Better keep us
> in dark ignorance, never to know anything, if you
> are going to refuse us the wherewithal to give ex-
> pression to those aspirations which have thus been
> created.*

In the Bristol dock strike of 1910, Bevin met an attempt
to use the unorganized carters to break the strike by organiz-
ing a carters' branch of the Dock, Wharf, Riverside and General Workers' Union. He soon became an investigator of complaints and working conditions for the union at £2 a week,
beginning a career as a belligerent trade union leader, which
took him to the very top of the British labor movement and
into the high command of the Trades Union Congress. In
the course of that career he fought unemployment, exploitation, employers, Communists, the British government itself
in the General Strike of 1926, and Fascism in England, Germany, and Italy. He organized the vast Transport and General Workers' Union. In May, 1940, upon the invitation of
his opponent in the General Strike, the Right Honorable
Winston Spencer Churchill, Prime Minister of a nation
fighting alone and sorely beset, he became Minister of
Labour and a member of the War Cabinet.

Bevin's reminiscences of the Dockers' Union were a delight. One day, talking about the Shaw Inquiry into conditions of labor on the docks (1920), he gave me a version of
an episode which differed from that recounted in Mr. Alan
Bullock's excellent biography. Mr. Bullock's version is taken
from the stenographic transcript. But Bevin, who in the

---

* *Ibid.*, pp. 125–26.

course of the inquiry became known as the "Dockers' K.C.," had over the years improved upon the record, as do all good advocates with their courtroom triumphs.

A Professor Bowley, an expert witness, had testified that £3.12.6 per week was a living wage for a family of five. Bevin put on the stand a burly docker, who, after testifying to the nature of a day's work on the docks, was shown a small plate on which was a dinner exactly as prescribed in the Bowley budget.

"Now, Joe," said the "Dockers' K.C.," "suppose you had just come home from work, and your good wife should set this dinner before you, what would you say?" The witness turned scarlet, seemed about to choke, and finally burst out, "I'd, I'd— Oh, for God's sake, Ernie!" At which Lord Shaw of Dunfermline intervened:

"Mr. Bevin, the record may show that the witness would express his disappointment and disapproval."

Regardless of truth, Bevin's recollection made a better story than the official record. Fortunately my own recollection of him does not face that stultifying corrective.

We soon became "Ernie" and "me lad," an affectionate appellation I shared with Mike Pearson (the Honorable Lester B. Pearson, then Canadian Secretary of State for External Affairs, now Leader of the Opposition). He and I agreed that one could catch Bevin's mood from his intonation of the phrase. It could be minatory, as in "And don't think, me lad, that I'm not on to what ye're up to." Or warmly reassuring, as when in 1950 Republican legislators were urging my replacement, "Don't give it a thought, me lad. If those blokes don't want yer, there's plenty as does."

Our work together that spring of 1949 laid a solid basis of trust and respect. Berlin raised no difficulties. Both Bevin and Schuman were relieved that the end of the blockade crisis was in sight, saw at once the need for our secret negotiations,

and approved the results we were working toward: the ending
of all restrictions and counter-restrictions—in other words,
the *status quo ante*—and, at Russian insistence, a Conference
of Foreign Ministers on German and Austrian questions.
After this, agreement with the Kremlin was reached and
simultaneous announcements prepared so swiftly and secretly
as to avoid the leaks, contradictory explanations, and embarrassing predictions which so often confuse joint action by
democratic allies. The meeting of Foreign Ministers was to
convene in Paris in May.

Agreement on the creation and form of a West German
government was a much harder problem. The experts on
the occupation staffs had introduced into the memoranda
prepared for us complexities of a formidable character. Men
who had spent four years creating these complexities, the
basis of their expertise, regarded them with immense serious-
ness. We were in the predicament of Mr. Joseph P. Cotton,
who, from 1929 to his death in 1931, was Under Secretary
of State in President Hoover's administration. An officer
came to him with a cable from one of our ambassadors asking
instructions about an intricate but unimportant issue raised
by a foreign government. "Oh," said Mr. Cotton, "tell him
to laugh it off." After a while the officer returned. "Mr.
Secretary," he said, "the code book has no word for 'laugh.' "

My confession to Schuman and Bevin of inability to understand these memoranda inclined them to regard me as an
honest man and a candid one. They made similar confessions.

The next step was to have prepared in simple language
a brief outline of a proposed new government, its powers,
duties, and limitations, and also of an agreement among
the three Allies on the operation by them of the powers
which they were to reserve. Bevin, Schuman, and I took the
papers off for study. At once what was really simple and

essential was revealed as such, and the true nature of the hard problems appeared.

These chiefly related to the operation of the reserved powers. Should German action stand unless reversed, or should it require affirmative approval? Should it be subject to veto by any one of the three occupying powers, or should a majority be required? One can easily imagine the agitation which these questions could arouse in 1949, and the problems of prestige. They were amicably settled by procedures which gave to the several High Commissioners suspensory vetoes, which could be dissolved by majority vote on appeal to the three governments. In practice I do not recall that many, if any, appeals were taken.

I mention these first problems, not because of their inherent interest or importance, but to underline that the trust and affection which grew out of our work together was not the product of a relaxed social and strifeless association.

The Conference of Foreign Ministers convened a few weeks later in Paris at the Palais Rose. This pink marble mansion on a street off the Champs-Élysées beyond the Arc de Triomphe had been built for Anna Gould when she was the bride of Boni de Castellane. As the Duchesse de Talleyrand-Périgord, she lent it in 1949 to the French Government. Its *fin de siècle* design and décor gave our wholly unreal meetings an incorrigible musical comedy setting and atmosphere. As we drove into its courtyard that first lovely May day and entered the rose marble hall, across which a wide double staircase rose to a mezzanine gallery, the Garde Républicaine's bugles and drums gave us flourishes and the Garde itself, in horsehair-plumed helmets, breastplates, white knee breeches, and high black boots, flashed its sabers in salute. One missed a rollicking opening chorus by Victor Herbert.

We met in what had been the dining room around a large,

circular, green-felt-covered table. Three pairs of French windows looked out on a garden containing one immense tree and many smaller flowering ones. The seats of the American delegation faced the garden. In the weeks that followed, its green depths and shadows soothed and refreshed spirits tortured by the excruciating boredom of hours of successive translations of everything said into two languages.

Above was a frescoed ceiling which took me back to my childhood. The fresco was of satyrs in hot pursuit of nymphs through clouds. In the center reclined a female figure, probably Aphrodite, an inattentive referee. When I was a child in Middletown, Connecticut, a similar scene, but with less purposeful pursuit and provocative flight by figures not yet called upon to discard so many hampering garments, was revealed with the rise of the asbestos curtain of the Macdonough Opera House.

The Palais Rose fresco got Bevin into trouble at our closing meeting. All meetings were strictly limited to the delegations and their staffs. But the last one being purely formal, I yielded to the pleas of my wife, Mrs. Bevin, and Mrs. David Bruce, the wife of our Ambassador, to smuggle them in to see a sight they had so often heard described. After proceedings had started, they slipped through a small serving door into seats held for them in the back of the room. Bevin was well into a speech thanking the municipal authorities of Paris and all their branches for their services to the conference. He was succeeding admirably in communicating his own boredom to his audience.

As the ladies came in, I made the mistake of a small gesture of greeting—mistaken, because Ernie, whose back was to them, thought I was signaling him to look upward. This he had not done before, since his short, stout neck was not naturally adapted to star-gazing. The fresco burst on him as an original discovery. His speech was just expressing per-

— Alors, vous verrez la vie en rose ?
— Quand vous cesserez d'être de marbre...

Cartoon which appeared in *Ici Paris*, May 30, 1949. By kind permission of the cartoonist, "bil."

functory appreciation of the facilities and hospitality of the
Palais Rose when the fresco opened new and unexpected
opportunities. He seized them with Rabelaisian gusto. Both
speaker and audience came to life. Laughter spurred him to
new effort, of which subtlety was not the chief element.

Matters were getting out of hand, and he could later on
believe, with some justification, that I had led him into a
trap. So I scribbled a note and tossed it across the table.
"Ernie: Flo is right behind you." With hardly a pause and
without turning around, he went on, "Well, as I was sayin',
we thank especially, etc., etc."

After the meeting, when tea was being served, I let him
get as far as, "Where you take your wife is your business, but
when it comes to takin' Flo . . ." I broke in, "By the way,
she's beckoning to us now. Let's join them," and moved off
to anchor under the guns of the fort.

To know Mrs. Bevin (now Dame Florence Bevin) was to
be devoted to her. There was no nonsense about her at all,
and great natural dignity. She gave the impression of straight-
forward, uncomplicated honesty like the couple in Grant
Wood's painting "American Gothic," an impression which
her long face and straight, bobbed gray hair, curled up at the
ends, reinforced. But there was nothing solemn about her,
except her concern for Ernie and their daughter. Hers was a
happy nature, joined with the gift of seeing through pretense,
without malice, in delighted amusement.

One evening in mid-June, when the conference was entering its fourth weary week and the mousy issue of its mountainous labor was becoming daily more evident, the Foreign
Ministers, High Commissioners, senior associates, and their
ladies were due to dine with Schuman in great style at the
Quai d'Orsay, the French Foreign Office. The dinner was for
eight o'clock in full evening dress. But the conference was
no respecter of such frivolities. It had entered the stage of

"secret" meetings, meetings limited to the Ministers, with one adviser each, and the interpreters. By a gentlemen's agreement, the press was not briefed on these meetings in the hope that a recess from propaganda might aid whatever chance there was of agreement. Secret meetings were a sure sign that, if the conference were to produce any result, high forceps would be required.

On the day of the dinner, the meeting began at three-thirty in the afternoon. At eight o'clock no end of the statements, counterstatements, and their infuriating translations seemed in sight. Schuman was unperturbed and unperturbable. A stream of messengers came to him and hastened off with scribbled notes. My heart ached for the chefs with their soups, fish, fowl, roasts, delicate vegetables, and salads, each course with its appropriate wine to be cooled, or brought to room temperature, at the exact moment. It was easy to forget the dreary, repetitive talk and wonder whether a series of dinners were being cooked and who would eat those which flowered too soon, or—though it did not seem possible—too late.

At last the interminable meeting ended. We reassembled about ten o'clock at the Quai d'Orsay, and sat down a half hour later. To my joy Mrs. Bevin was on my left. At once we made a conversational deal. We were too exhausted, hungry, and murderously inclined, we agreed, for most topics. Only fantasy of the purest gossamer would do. What should it be? She looked across and down the long table and fastened on a lady toward the other end, dressed, as the expression goes, to the nines; of just what period was not too clear.

"I know," she said triumphantly. "Let's talk about why women like to wear feathers in their hair."

"But do they, really?" I asked. "Isn't it only when they're presented at court?"

"Not a bit of it. I've always longed to, but 'e (with a glance across the table at Ernie) won't let me."

"Why on earth not?" I asked. But the glance had had telepathic result.

"What're you two talkin' about?" Ernie broke in from his place opposite. "What won't I let 'er do? Fat chance of that!"

"Pay no attention to him," I said. "We oughtn't to encourage him to talk across the table and neglect those nice ladies beside him." (One of them was my wife.)

"I think it's very bad manners," Flo added.

"You're puttin' 'er up to something," said Ernie.

"Flo," I went on, "I've been thinking about those feathers. Do you suppose your longing for them is some instinct inherited from a distant ancestor of ours beyond the veil of time, who was also an ancestor of the birds?"

"Oh, my God!" came from across the table.

"'E'll never let us alone," said Flo. "Talk to your neighbor and we'll go on later." This we did, watched suspiciously through dinner.

The next morning he came up to me before the CFM. "You and your damned birds," he said, and went into the meeting room.

The conference encountered heavy weather from the start. The Russians plainly had no intention of making any agreement for German unity which would weaken their hold on the Eastern Zone. Any agreement at all which did not put all Germany under Soviet control would do this, since the Russians were hated and feared in East Germany, and the German Communists were despised as traitors. So the meetings were given over to propaganda statements and maneuvers, such as Vyshinsky's proposal to withdraw all troops from Germany in 1950 and to call a conference in Paris to write a peace treaty for Germany.

It was soon apparent that we had a more serious issue to face than the mere failure of the conference. Failure had been almost inherent in its purpose—saving face for the

Cartoon by Curry from *Franc-Tireur*, Paris, June 7, 1949, entitled *"Le Quadrille Du Palais Rose"*; (l. to r.) Ernest Bevin, the author, Robert Schuman, Andrei Vyshinsky.

Russian decision to abandon the blockade. But we soon discovered that they had not wholly abandoned it. The Commandants reported from Berlin that no rail traffic was moving because of a strike on the Russian-operated railroad in West Berlin due to the refusal of the Russian management to pay Western Sector rail workers in West marks, the Eastern marks offered being worth one-fourth as much. Furthermore, the Russian Commandant had brought the process of removing restrictions on trade to an impasse.

Here, plainly, was a test of resolution. Some within our own American group, of whom Foster Dulles was one, believed we should vigorously protest to Moscow about this, but not endanger the conference. I was delighted to find that neither Bevin nor Schuman shared this view. We three were agreed that the conference was conditioned on the complete and immediate ending of the blockade. If that condition was not met, the conference would end.

With the approval of our governments, we demanded that Vyshinsky join with us in instructions to the Commandants to conclude their negotiations and get traffic moving in three days. At first he refused; but, seeing that we were quite serious about ending the conference, reversed his position on the basis of new information just received. Someone suggested that it must have been an invisible note brought by an invisible pigeon. At all events progress began again; and, though it took more than three days to work out all the problems of Berlin traffic, it was done.

"Comfortable," in the Elizabethan use, means reassuring. I felt then, as throughout our time together, what comfortable men I had to work with in the bluff English labor leader and the retiring, ascetic Lorraine lawyer.

The conference ground to its end on June 20, 1949. Little was decided about Germany. We tried and failed to get a physical corridor from Helmstedt to Berlin. But a *modus vivendi* of sorts was worked out on trade and traffic with Berlin, and general undertakings were made of mild and transitory benefit. Rather surprising progress was made on a treaty for an independent Austria. After many hundreds of sterile meetings by the deputies, the ice seemed to melt. We came within a stone's throw of the result finally achieved in 1955. But the northern night descended to undo our work, as I shall tell.

At six o'clock on Monday evening, June 20, the conference adjourned *sine die,* with the ceremonies already described. After a final glass of champagne and polite farewells around the buffet tables, we parted, Bevin for an early dinner and the boat-train for London. At our Embassy, in the course of the liturgical ending of all endeavors, a press conference, word came to me that an emergency meeting of the CFM had been called by Schuman at the Quai d'Orsay within the hour, at the request of Vyshinsky. No reason had been given. This news broke up the press meeting. While we ate a hurried sandwich, we learned through our French friends that Gromyko, Vyshinsky's Deputy Foreign Minister, had telephoned him from Moscow after the adjournment and in most brutal language told him that his agreements on Austria were unsatisfactory in omitting an important provision and must be reopened.

Bevin and I reached the Quai d'Orsay together. On the way up the steps I gave him my report, which accorded with his.

"Any ideas?" he asked.

"I'd tell him to go to hell."

"Me, too," he agreed.

In the Quai d'Orsay's glass-enclosed elevator, which shook and protested under our combined weight, Ernie asked, "Do you know our labor song, 'The Red Flag'?" I had to confess ignorance. "The tune's the same as 'Maryland, My Maryland.' Y' know that, coming from there? Let's sing 'em together, as a sign of solidarity, as we labor blokes say."

And so we did, robustly, arm-in-arm, walking through the sedate Second Empire anterooms, with the final bars at the very entrance of the meeting room. As a mark of solidarity it was impressive.

We had barely a word with Schuman before Vyshinsky reported Moscow's demand that the protocol which he had signed be reopened to provide for the payment to the USSR of "profits and other income" in convertible currency.

Vyshinsky was unable to explain the scope of this provision or the need for it. He was unwilling to leave the matter for our deputies to explore.

Bevin congratulated him on a new record. Soviet agreements were fragile things, but today's was the frailest yet. It had not even survived the day. However, he saw no reason to reconsider our adjournment, or change our words. Schuman and I briefly agreed. The meeting adjourned. By midnight the lights of Paris and then London disappeared behind us as the *Independence* gained altitude on her northerly course back to Washington. I thought with affection of the "comfortable" and stalwart friends I had just left.

Bevin came back to Washington in the autumn of 1949, accompanied by Sir Stafford Cripps, the Chancellor of the Exchequer, and a group of Treasury officials. He had a long agenda before him—Britain's serious financial troubles, talks with the French and us, a NATO Council meeting, and the General Assembly of the United Nations—a heavy schedule for a man far from well.

I was interested to see him perform with Cripps. Bevin had told me that after the Labour victory in 1945 he had wanted, and rather expected, to be Chancellor of the Exchequer. He had long been a student of national finance and its relation to Britain's national economy and international trade and financial position. His knowledge was respected; his claims were strong. The offer of the Foreign Office was a disappointment. But it was like him to accept the decision in good spirit and make the most of it.

It was like him, too, to study not only current international problems, but the history of his office and the history of his predecessors. He read their papers; he talked of them as of slightly older people whom he knew with affectionate respect. In listening to him, one felt strongly the continuity and integrity of English history. He conferred a single title on each of them. It was "Old." "Last night," he said to me, "I was readin' some papers of Old Salisbury. Y' know 'e 'ad a lot of sense." "Old Palmerston," too, came in for frequent, and sometimes wistful, mention. One got the sense that, sitting at the familiar desk, under the portrait of George III, he felt himself surrounded by their benign shades, sympathizing with him in his worries, which had been essentially theirs, too— problems too large for the means readily available—and saying to him, "Good man, Bevin! We know how it is."

With George III he was very companionable. When sherry was brought in before lunch, he would twist around to look up at the portrait. "Let's drink to 'im," he would say. "If 'e 'adn't been so stoopid, you wouldn't 'ave been strong enough to come to our rescue in the war, and after it with Marshall aid." His Majesty, I think, was not amused.

I thought again, the following May, of the flow of English history and how fitting it was for Bevin to take his place in it, when he gave a dinner and reception for the NATO Foreign Ministers at St. James's Palace. That Tudor setting was just right for Bevin in scale and taste. When, after dinner, the uniformed "toastmaster" beat on the floor with his staff for quiet, and announced, "Your Grace, Your Excellencies, My Lords and Ladies, ladies and gentlemen, pray silence for His Majesty's Secretary of State for Foreign Affairs, the Right Honorable Ernest Bevin," I could believe that a Tudor monarch could well have seen in the short, powerful figure who rose to welcome us an instrument well fashioned to safeguard English interests.

I have wandered far from our financial conference of 1949.

Cripps I had known for some fifteen years. A barrister, at one time the leader of the bar, he brought his disciplined analytical mind to the Treasury with results which seemed painfully conservative and ascetic to some of his Labour colleagues, of whom Aneurin Bevan was one. The mention of

the name tempts me to another digression. It is said that
hearing someone repeat the cliché, "Nye Bevan is his own
worst enemy," Ernie broke in emphatically, "Not while I'm
alive."

Cripps and Bevin were a formidable team. We had antici-
pated their arrival with much speculation among State,
Treasury, and Federal Reserve Board as to whether the
British would want to discuss devaluation of the pound
sterling and what our attitude should be. Financial people
are curiously timid. Their attitude here, that even to discuss
devaluation both incurred a commitment to underwrite the
result and made us accessory to a possible outbreak of financial hostilities, seemed to me sterile and negative. But the
financiers were leading in these talks and their attitude
colored our preparations.

When the moment arrived, Cripps and Bevin did not seek
our advice about a decision to be made, but told us about a
decision which had been made. To a very small group and,
of course, in deepest secrecy, they told us that the value of
the pound would be halved as soon as they had the necessary
talks at the International Monetary Fund. This was promptly
done. The fact that it was done in Washington and with our
obvious knowledge inevitably led to a larger role being im-
puted to us than the facts warranted. But I pointed out to
my querulous brethren in the Treasury that we would have
been vastly annoyed if we had not been told in advance, and
that it was not due to British insistence that the headquarters
of the Bank and Fund were in Washington.

Our talks, then, were on steps to be taken after devaluation,
not about its wisdom. Stafford Cripps's patience was short
and his temper quick. John Snyder, Secretary of the Treasury,
who chaired the meetings, seemed to exhaust the former and
arouse the latter. Stafford would become waspish and often
stung. Sometimes the whole hive swarmed angrily out. Here,

as so often happens, Bevin, a quick-tempered man himself, took on a benevolent objectivity and became the peacemaker, using me as a sort of end man in his diversionary tactic.

But his contribution was more than to smooth a rough place. He seemed to have cornered the market for common sense. I have heard it said that Paul Hoffman, the administrator of the Marshall Plan, missed his calling: that he should have been an evangelist. Both statements miss the truth. He didn't miss his calling, and he was and is an evangelist. At one of our meetings he was preaching to the British his doctrine of salvation by exports with all the passion of an economic Savonarola. The British were following, he said, the false course of exporting to soft currency countries for high prices; and getting full employment, but no gold or dollars. They must take the harder road of reducing costs and exporting to the American dollar market.

Bevin mildly suggested that the British had tried this course in the twenties and their very success had gotten them the Smoot-Hawley Tariff Act and lost them their American markets. Americans liked to talk about trade replacing aid, until imports began; then called for "peril points" and "escape clauses" against the competition of "cheap labor." When Hoffman attributed this talk to the days before the Enlightenment, Bevin was as well prepared as any lawyer with the history of increasing limitations put on each extension of the Trade Agreements Act, which, although first enacted fifteen years before, was still regarded as temporary commercial policy and extended only a few years, sometimes only a year, at a time. He spoke with good nature, but great force; and he was entirely right.

Bevin, as has been said, was far from well in the autumn of 1949. He gave us a good fright after we had moved to New York for the General Assembly of the United Nations. On our second evening there my wife and I took him to *South*

Pacific with Ambassador-at-large and Mrs. Philip Jessup. Mrs. Bevin had gone off to visit friends in the country. As we sat in the front row, the orchestra recognized Ernie at once and the word went backstage. Pinza, Mary Martin, and the whole cast played to him. He enjoyed himself so obviously and so expansively that actors and audience caught his gaiety. It was a joyous evening.

Our security guards, including Scotland Yard Inspector "Big Ben" Macey, advised staying in our seats between the acts, which gave Bevin several hours of inactivity. After a tumultuous final curtain, with many calls, and much waving by and to him, we started to follow the departing audience up the aisle. The sudden demand on his heart brought on an attack. Inspector Macey took command in an instant. Ernie was stretched in the aisle with sweat pouring down his face. A towel soaked in icewater was brought to cool his face, nitroglycerine administered. The police emptied the theater; but the crowd waited outside.

We waited in the back of the theater, but not for long. The pain passed. Ernie soon joined us, with apologies for frightening everyone. As we came out of the theater and got into our cars, the crowd gave him a cheer and got a gay wave back.

"Where are we goin' now?" he asked when the cars moved off.

"We're going back to the hotel to see that you go to bed," I told him, not adding that his devoted private secretary, Roddie Barclay, and the hotel doctor were awaiting him.

"*Then* what are you goin' to do?" he persisted.

"Probably take the Jessups up to our apartment for a nightcap before we turn in."

"I thought so," he said triumphantly. "And I'm comin', too. You're not goin' to tuck me in. I need a drink more than any of you."

"It isn't good for him, is it?" I appealed to Inspector Macey. "He'd much better go to bed. Isn't that right, Inspector?"

"Well, sir," said "Big Ben" from the front seat, "I don't rightly know what's best for him. But I've a fair idea of what he's going to do."

And so he did. We went along to our apartment, where Barclay and the doctor came to receive and give reassurance. Then, gaining the former as a recruit, we had an hour of animated discussion of the play. Bevin was indomitable and made no concessions to weaknesses of the flesh.

Later that same autumn I was to learn that failing health had in no way weakened his redoubtable temper. In November we met in Paris with Schuman; the subject German steel production. At the end of the war severe decisions had been taken to insure against future German aggression by dismantling a large part of the German steel industry. As the Marshall Plan got under way, dismantling was increasingly revealed as an impediment to industrial recovery in Europe. A study by Mr. George Humphrey, later Secretary of the Treasury, demonstrated the need for a change of policy, and pointed out the anomaly of the United States supplying the German economy with steel which it could make itself.

At our spring meeting with the British and French Foreign Ministers we had drawn up a final list of plants to be dismantled and had agreed that German steel production would not be permitted above a specified tonnage figure to be enforced by the allied control authority in the Ruhr. By October dismantling had become an acute and open issue. The Bonn government was protesting against the program of dismantling. German workers were threatening to refuse to work at it. Most of the plants on the list for removal were in the British Zone of Occupation so that the German

criticisms were chiefly directed against the British government. The British believed that the dismantling policy must
be modified but also believed that German steel production
must not be unrestricted. The United States government
favored going somewhat further than the British. The French
were opposed to any liberalization whatever. Here was a
tinderbox waiting for a spark.

It had not long to wait. Our High Commissioner to Germany, Mr. John J. McCloy, supplied it. Mr. McCloy belongs
in the first rank of men with whom I have worked. He came
to the War Department, at Secretary Henry L. Stimson's call,
from a successful New York legal practice to serve as Assistant
Secretary during the Second World War, having been an
artilleryman in the First. In 1947, President Truman put
him forward to be President of the International Bank for
Reconstruction and Development, and as soon as civilian
high commissioners replaced military governors in Western
Germany, the President sent him there. The fundamental
quality in McCloy's nature is vitality, a rare and priceless
gift. He never tires, never flags. His mind stays fresh, imaginative, and vigorous throughout a whole night of complex negotiation. Physically he bounces. Jack McCloy has
been known to wear to tatters two pairs of socks during a
tennis match, a game at which he excels. A man of this temperament is forthright. Where security is necessary, he can
keep quiet; but if an argument is going on, his views are
pretty likely to pop out.

And this is just what they did in October, 1949. He spoke
his mind on the subject of dismantling. It accorded pretty
well with the mind of his government, though more strik-
ingly expressed than an official statement would have been,
if there had been one—which there had not. These differences
we had been trying to work out in private.

These statements dismayed the French and infuriated

Bevin. Though not intended to do so, they made him appear the obstruction to German aspirations, made the whole matter more difficult to work out with the Germans, and appeared to Bevin to give McCloy some sort of supranational authority which Bevin was not ready to concede. On the contrary he thought that he recognized pressure tactics and resented them passionately. When we met in Paris in November, he burned in the white heat of his rage.

The moment Schuman opened the meeting, Bevin let us have it with both barrels. His excoriation of international negotiation by use of the press was a masterpiece of truth and vituperation. Beating the air with both arms, he worked himself into a passion, which, after our New York experience, filled me with concern for him. But he soon tired, and surprised us by coming to a sudden stop, and asking me what I had to say.

What, indeed? Schuman looked at me appealingly. Ernie was getting his breath for a second round. There was no defense and to attempt one would only make matters worse. The problem was to make forgiveness possible before asking for it. The key lay in Ernie's sense of humor. Then it was that my youth in a rectory and a church school came to my rescue.

"*M. le Président*," I said to Schuman, "all that I can reply to Mr. Bevin is written in an English book, *The Book of Common Prayer:* 'The remembrance of our sins is grievous unto us; the burden of them is intolerable.' "

Waving aside translation, Schuman eagerly interjected, "It is the same in the Catholic book." Ernie burst into laughter and threw up his arms in mock despair.

"I wouldn't know," he said. "I'm only a bush Baptist."

"What in the world," I asked, "is a *bush* Baptist?"

"I don't know," he answered. "That's what they called us. Why don't you ask your President? 'e's probably one, too."

I said that I would; and later did. (I find this postscript to a letter I wrote Bevin on November twenty-first after returning home: "The authority on Baptists, Mr. H.S.T., says that in the early days the mountain people went for the principles of the Baptists in a big way, as they were regarded as a protest against the decadence of the cities. A 'bush Baptist' was a Baptist from the hills.")

But the storm had passed. Bevin good-naturedly accepted our contrite apologies and assurances that, for a time at least, members of the American delegation would check their inclination to regard a question from the press as compulsive, as one from St. Peter at the Pearly Gates.

The next day his tolerance of tiresome nagging was put to the test. While the difficulty over our High Commissioner's statements was fairly easily solved, the problem of German steel was much harder. We had set aside only two days for it, with the result that on the second day our sessions lasted from 10 A.M. to 4 the next morning; with two ceremonial meals thrown in. This was a pretty rugged schedule for a man with Bevin's ailment. Luncheon was at the Quai d'Orsay—as elaborate as it was delicious, liberally sprinkled with wines. After lunch Bevin, Schuman, and I were standing together when coffee and liqueurs were passed. Ernie took some brandy then handed the glass to me to hold while he put sugar in a demitasse. I put the brandy back on the waiter's tray.

"Mr. Bevin has changed his mind," I said to the waiter. "He isn't going to have any brandy, and I don't think that he is going to have any coffee either." With that I took the coffee cup from him and returned it to the tray.

"Of all the insufferable . . . !" Ernie began. I turned to Schuman and asked him whether he could reserve one of those French hearses with black angels at the four corners, drawn by black-plumed horses, and driven by silk-hatted coachmen with caped overcoats.

Schuman said, "Yes, but why?"

"Mr. Bevin," I said, "is apparently thinking of giving a party at which he is likely to be the central figure, and he may need one of them. And, by the way, have you a room with a couch where he could take a nap?"

"Damn it," snapped Ernie, "will you mind your own business."

"Surely," I answered. "As the saying goes, it's your own funeral. But I will go to it." Schuman added that that was true for him also—he would regret it, but he would go.

"Oh," said Bevin resignedly, "where's the couch?" Schuman took him to it. He stretched out and slept. Later, as the night of discussion and compromise wore on, I did not regret my officiousness; nor, do I think, did he.

When I saw Bevin again in May, 1950, he had failed perceptibly, weakened by a painful operation. One afternoon in his own office he keeled over onto the table, partly from exhaustion, partly from the sedatives he had to take. He was better in the autumn in New York for a NATO meeting and the UN General Assembly. Then he stood stalwartly by me in a most difficult time.

The course of Soviet policy and the military weakness of the NATO Allies were making plain the necessity for collective defense organization, strategy, and command in the defense of Europe. The attack on South Korea added urgency. The NATO meeting in May, with France in the forefront, had agreed upon the principle of collective defense. Soon afterward the French circulated far-reaching memoranda on a common defense budget and organization. In the United States the Pentagon raised the relevant point that a unified defense of Europe was not possible unless Western Germany, the keystone geographically and militarily, were a part of it.

This was indisputable. But there could be and was a difference of opinion on how to bring it about. The Pentagon insisted on making German participation a condition to a unified command, on the logically persuasive ground that the command would be an American responsibility and should not be assumed until it was made feasible by German participation. The State Department argued that only the logic of demonstrated necessity would gain French agreement to German rearmament. German participation was bound to follow the establishment of the unified command. If it did not, the United States could and should withdraw from the command. Time, we argued, was essential to accustom the French to the idea of military association with Germany.

This is not the place to go into the history of the unified command and the common defense of Europe. That tangled skein is still being unwound. It is enough to say that the command was finally established in accordance with the State Department prescription, but not until the Pentagon's plan had been tried on and produced a Donnybrook, in which many heads were broken and tempers and time lost. During this trying experience Bevin held out a sympathetic and helping hand.

That this misguided effort was largely my own fault did not make it any easier. The United States government was not agreed on the Pentagon plan until early September, only a day or two before Bevin sailed for New York. By this time the usual leaks had opened it to press speculation. Deciding that there was no practical alternative to going ahead at the meetings in New York, we sent word to Bevin and Schuman of what was afoot so that they might have, at least, some consultations before setting out. But everything was wrong: the plan itself, the attempt to bring it forward without preparation. Perhaps the Pentagon divined my better judgment; they sent along a mentor to see that German participation never became separated from the unified command. A very pleasant person he was, still a good friend, Admiral Thomas H. Robbins, Jr., then known as "One Package Robbins."

Bevin was strong for the purpose and doubtful of the method. His government had more extensive doubts, but he got Shinwell, the Minister of Defence, to fly over and worked the government around to supporting our proposal. He doubtless told them that they could do this with little risk, since the French could be counted on to block all action for quite a while. But he was nonetheless a stout ally, since all the while the idea of doing something was gaining general acceptance, even in France.

"Y've got the right idea, me lad," Ernie would say, "but"—with a chuckle—"you do go about it the hard way."

The French were adamant in their opposition to our original proposal. First the tripartite meeting and then the NATO meeting could make no progress. General Marshall, who became Secretary of Defense in the middle of the battle and joined me in New York, agreed that we should break off the effort and try another approach. With his invaluable help this was done, and the unified command was established in December, 1950, with General Eisenhower as Supreme Commander, and with German participation subject to further consideration.

Bevin had a deep mistrust of the Germans, but an even deeper one of the Soviet Union. And he understood power. He knew that choices had to be made, often choices between unpleasant alternatives, and never was misled, as so many well-meaning people are, into believing that the necessity for choice can be transcended by a flight of eloquence. He profoundly believed that the possibility of life in freedom anywhere depended on the United States and the United Kingdom sticking together. Not that they could preserve freedom by themselves, or wanted to do so only for themselves, but he was sure that it couldn't be done anywhere for long if they drifted apart.

He knew too that, because our two countries were united on the basic values by which they lived, it did not necessarily follow that all their interests were identical. So, though he urged strongly that we act together in recognizing the Communist government of China at the end of 1949, he came to see that the problems and interests of our two governments were different and would not be served by parallel action. We could and did take different roads without irritation or strain.

In short, Bevin held strongly to certain principles, which for his time were as important as they were valid. They were not "a body of principle," rather separate convictions leaving room for interstitial flexibility and empirical operation. This capacity in a colleague is a great comfort in dealing with events which refuse to conform to patterns. He was firm about the main things and willing to improvise about lesser matters. I come back to the idea that he was a "comfortable" man to work with.

Unhappily the time left to us was all too short. On March 9, 1951, he could go on no longer. "I stuck the job as long as I could," he wrote in answer to my note of regret when he resigned. A month later he was dead. In sorrow and affection I said of him:

> Ernest Bevin's death brings to me deep sorrow from the loss of a friend and trusted colleague. We have worked together for two and one half years in a critical and troubled time, sharing common problems and determined in the interests of our countries to find solutions in common. To work with him inevitably evoked deep affection, respect, and

trust. It could not be otherwise, because his indomitable courage, his simplicity and directness, his love of his country and his understanding of the grandeur of its contribution to the cause of human liberty, his humanity and knowledge of the struggles and aspirations of his fellowmen, his own warm affectionate good humor made him both loved and trusted.

We have sat together in many international conferences and personal meetings. We have exchanged innumerable messages on the problems confronting us. He fought hard for views which were always founded on a remarkable knowledge of history, an apprehension—deeper than knowledge—that he was acting in the moving stream of history, and an understanding of present facts. But his mind was not closed. It was tough, and often stubborn, but always open to arguments strongly and honestly pushed.

Not only his own countrymen, but all of us to whom freedom and liberty are the foundation of our lives will stand in spirit beside his grave in sorrow and gratitude and joy that in these times such a man has lived.

Ernest Bevin was a gallant gentleman, a great Englishman, a fighter for the freedom of all men.

II

ROBERT SCHUMAN

French Premier, 1947–1948
French Foreign Minister, 1948–1953

Robert Schuman was as different from Ernest Bevin in appearance, temperament, mind, and manner as a man could be. A lean man, slightly stooped, his long, serious, even ascetic face gives an appearance of baffled solemnity, enhanced by the bald dome and his habit of sinking chin in collar to peer over the top of his spectacles. He speaks quietly, often in the abstract generalizations natural to lawyers trained in the civil law. His sense of humor is keen, but almost furtive, wholly different from Bevin's broad and rollicking gaiety.

I remember sitting beside him one evening in February, 1952, at a men's dinner of Eden's during the four-power meetings. M. François-Poncet, French High Commissioner to Germany, was on my other side; Chancellor Adenauer, across the table. The two were discussing the hazards which lurk in memoirs.

"I will be generous to you in my memoirs," said Adenauer to François-Poncet, "if you will be the same to me in yours." François-Poncet agreed. Schuman leaned over to me.

"Adenauer will lose," he murmured. "He will die first."

Born in Luxembourg in 1886, Schuman grew up and was educated in Lorraine when it was part of Germany, so completely at home in both French and German that in our meetings with Adenauer he would quite unconsciously begin a reply to the Chancellor in German without waiting for the translation which protocol required. Then he would stop with a guilty smile and wave the interpreter on.

Schuman's manner was formal, dignified, and gravely courteous. Whereas Bevin and I were soon on a first-name basis, Schuman to the end of our association called me "Mr. Acheson," and I addressed him as "M. Schuman," or *"M. le Président,"* since he had been Premier, President of the Council of Ministers, in 1947–48. But beneath this formality was a nature warm and affectionate to those to whom he gave his confidence, feelings which shyness rarely let show through the protective cover.

But there was steel in him, too. Under his premiership, the Communists were thrown out of the governing coalition and a beginning was made on eliminating party members from the "sensitive" areas of the bureaucracy. He could be as adamant as Molotov when he thought that the interests of France or the necessities of French politics required it, but never in the Molotov manner. He simply withdrew behind walls of impenetrable logic glazed with courtesy.

It was said, though I cannot vouch for it, that his almost monkish asceticism led him, while Foreign Minister, to live in a few rooms over his offices in the Quai d'Orsay, attended only by an old woman who had been his nurse. Like many spiritual and cultivated men, Schuman's character and his beliefs were essentially simple. A devout Christian and Catholic, a true patriot, he believed Edith Cavell's statement that "patriotism is not enough."

Essential to an understanding of Schuman's thought is the fact that he was a man of the border. He grew up, studied law and began its practice in Metz under German rule. In 1919 he was elected to the French National Assembly from the Department of Moselle. The experiences and impressions of his early life were like those of two other border men, Abraham Lincoln and Andrew Johnson. Like them, he learned that only in reconciliation and larger loyalties could the people of half a continent find a happier and more fruitful life. His task, as he saw it, was to bring France and Germany together so that they might lead Europe to unity within a still broader Atlantic community. No aim could have been more congenial to me.

The instability of governments under the Fourth Republic is often cited as evidence or cause of its weakness, and with much justice. During my four years as Secretary of State, France had six governments. On the other hand, Robert Schuman's tenure at the Quai d'Orsay almost exactly coincided with mine at the State Department. His began in July, 1948; mine, in January, 1949. We both left office in January, 1953.

Schuman had his vision of a unified Europe at a time when it was hard to have vision in France, and did his work in a place where it was difficult to work. France was in the grip of an inferiority neurosis, and the Quai d'Orsay was deeply divided by strong personalities, some favoring, some disapproving the trend of Schuman's thought—Hervé Alphand, Maurice Couve de Murville, Alexandre Parodi, Maurice Schumann. Conspiratorial habits formed during the war and in the resistance persisted in the Quai d'Orsay. This limited the help available to Schuman. It was perhaps well that he was by nature a solitary worker, for he had to be careful who knew what he was thinking about before he was ready to act.

Schuman's progress in English was a touching measure of the growth of our friendship. Happily he had never been taught English as I had been taught French. Years and years of it had drilled me in the now forgotten complexities of French grammar and French irregular verbs. My reading French, once excellent, has suffered with the years. And spoken French, which always seems to be at machine-gun speed, reduces me to panic. My attempts to reply cause every Frenchman to take on the look of a mastiff trying to overlook the impertinences of a fox terrier. The French resent the efforts of barbarians to address them in what the lesser breeds hopefully believe to be the French language. Italians, on the other hand, greet even the most depressing efforts to speak Italian with unrestrained enthusiasm. They are naturally kindly people.

Schuman was even more kindly. He worked hard at his English, until, after a time, he could dispense with translation in informal talk. Usually, however, we had an interpreter at hand because, although he made great progress at understanding, he had the familiar trouble in expressing himself in the foreign language. He flattered me by saying that for the most part he could understand me since I spoke slowly and clearly. But Bevin's West Country and Anthony Eden's Etonian-Oxford English always remained incomprehensible to him. This was not, of course, true of Eden's excellent French.

One evening, in the autumn of 1949, during the United Nations General Assembly meeting in New York, my wife and I put his English to a severe test. After dining together, we went to Cole Porter's delightful musical comedy *Kiss Me, Kate*. Dinner was easy, and at first the play delighted him. Being a Shakespeare lover, he recognized *The Taming of the Shrew* and loved the music. Then things began to get mixed up. The play within the play, the intrusion of the gangster theme, both convinced him that he had missed something. He asked us to explain. Neither of us could, since we were as thoroughly confused as he. Our efforts to explain that we could not explain, and why, got everyone beyond his depth in both languages. In the end members of his staff, some days later, straightened us all out. For weeks he would shake his head over the complexity of the whole idea.

I worked with Schuman for a year and came to like and admire him before I glimpsed the magnitude of his imagination and originality. The discovery came through an experience which got us both into trouble with Bevin.

A meeting of NATO's Council of Ministers had been arranged for early May, 1950, in London. Bevin, Schuman, and I were to have a day or so together first. Since all of this was to be in London, some of my colleagues advised that it would be courteous to go to London via Paris and have informal talks there. So I did, getting there Sunday morning, May 7. Ambassador David Bruce met me at Orly, and here I must pause to say a word about this friend and colleague.

Not often has high position and responsibility so insistently sought out a man as has been the case with David Bruce; and not one of his posts has he sought himself. Beginning as a career diplomat, he was soon lured away by business, war, and administration in government. He served as Under Secretary of Commerce and, later, as deputy to Mr. Harriman in supervising the operation of the Marshall Plan in Europe. Then three Presidents claimed him for even greater responsibility. President Truman sent him to France as our Ambassador; President Eisenhower, to Germany; and now (1961) President Kennedy has appointed him Ambassador in London. If anyone has ever faulted him in any of these assignments, I do not know of it, or of pressure or weariness ever moving him from his gentle and humorous good nature. Most of the time covered here, he and his equally gifted wife continually sustained and guided me in their hospitable Paris house. Then, much against their preference, they came back to Washington to see me through my final year of office. Perhaps this action suggests those qualities of integrity, loyalty, and honor which have caused so many high positions to seek this man.

But to return to Paris in 1950, on the drive into town Bruce told me that Schuman would call on me at the Ambassador's residence. Only Bruce, Schuman, his interpreter, and I were to be present. This was puzzling. The request had come when Bruce had asked for an appointment for me to pay my respects to Schuman at the Quai d'Orsay on Monday morning. We racked our brains to think of any reason for a Sunday call.

We soon found out. After a few words of greeting and appreciation of my coming to Paris, Schuman began to expound what later became known as the "Schuman Plan," so breathtaking a step toward the unification of Western Europe that at first I did not grasp it. The whole French-German production of coal and steel would be placed under a joint high authority, with an organization open to the participation of other European nations. Schuman implored us to treat what he was about to tell us in the greatest confidence, not to speak to any of our colleagues about it, not to send cables, or to have memoranda transcribed. For he had discussed the proposal only with the Premier and one or two members of the Cabinet. The next step would be to consult the whole Cabinet, and, if it approved, then to make some public statement, perhaps in the Chamber of Deputies. After that, France's neighbors would be approached. A leak of any sort before the French government was aligned could wreck the plan and destroy the government. Schuman wanted to give me time to consider the proposal carefully and understand its full implications, for he believed that it was wholly in accord with American policy. The strong support of our government would be invaluable.

As Schuman talked, I was impressed, as I was so often to be, by his simple approach to a big idea, a far cry from that of American-trained lawyers. He stuck entirely to the broad, central principle, expounding that. We would complicate it by elaborating ideas on organization and procedure as well as safeguards against real and imagined dangers.

Almost my first thought was along this line, that the arrangement could become a giant cartel controlling the basic necessities of an industrial society. A policy of our occupation in Germany had been to break up these cartels. I put the danger to Schuman. The question surprised and rather offended him. Of course, a cartel in coal and steel could be created, he answered. But his purpose, which he had tried to make clear, was very different. It was basically a political conception: to move toward the unification of Western Europe by economic means. Surely, provisions would be made against cartel abuses and for a court to enforce them. He treated my fear almost as an irrelevance, as back he went to the central theme, the unity of Europe, the end of national rivalries in a new, spacious, and vastly productive Europe. As he talked, we caught his enthusiasm and the breadth of his thought, the rebirth of Europe, which, as an entity, had been in eclipse since the Reformation.

We parted with his promise to have Jean Monnet go further with us into the details of the plan and its proposed execution, and our promise to keep silent. Bruce and I were left to ponder our duty and our course. Fortunately they flowed together, at least to begin with. While our first impression of the plan had been highly favorable, we must clearly know much more before we could advise the President to support it. In response to an inquiry "in clear" we learned that the President had gone to the West in his train to dedicate a dam. Plainly a communication to the train was too hazardous. So there was time to learn, and no conflict between duty and the obligation to keep Schuman's confidence.

With Monnet, one of France's most able economist-states-
men, as teacher, and High Commissioner (to Germany)
McCloy, whom Monnet had brought into the cabal, to put
some of Monnet's vagueness into political institutions of a
sort, we made headway fast. Our confidence in the plan grew
with our education, though much of it remained nebulous.
Our first "eyes only" cable to the President said only that
an important development might (repeat might) take place
within a few days, which I was confident the President would
favor and on which further information would be available
soon. In the meantime, should rumors begin to come from
Europe, would he please withhold comment until I could
inform him further. He replied that he would. The danger
was that the first report of the plan would arouse fears in the
Departments of Justice and Commerce similar to my own
first thoughts and someone might shoot from the hip.

Before flying to London two days later and after learning
that the French Cabinet had acted favorably on the plan, we
sent another "eyes only" message outlining the plan, urging
that on its announcement I be permitted to express warm
and sympathetic interest pending further elaboration from
Paris, and that until its announcement the information be
kept secret. The President approved.

In London Bevin was ill and, understandably, testy. On
the morning of my arrival I met with him but did not feel
free to mention Schuman's plan. At lunch at Bevin's house
a message was brought to him that M. Massigli, the French
Ambassador, was asking for an appointment with Bevin
right after lunch and with me an hour later. He wondered
what was up. I did not. The call, of course, was to tell us
that Schuman was unveiling his plan that afternoon and to
outline it.

I kept a four o'clock appointment at the Foreign Office
with dragging feet. Bevin asked me to see him alone. He was

in a towering rage, and at once charged that I had known of
Schuman's plan and had kept it from him. This, of course,
was true and I said so. But, before I could explain, he rushed
on to accuse me of having conspired with Schuman to create
a European combination against British trade with the continent. This was quite untrue, but I had certainly behaved
suspiciously. And, since he would not listen, I could not
explain the circumstantial evidence against me. Why would
an honest man have gone from Washington to London via
Paris at this precise moment?

It took a long time to reduce his blood pressure to the
point where discussion would replace denunciation. Then,
though he would not acquit me of conspiracy, he gave me a
Scotch verdict of "not proven." I agreed that he had a cause
of complaint in the shortness of his notice. Finally we took
up what we should say about the plan to the hovering press.
A joint statement was impossible since he bristled with hos-
tility to Schuman's whole idea. I thought a little gentle bully-
ing was now needed and dropped the idea that, as his
statement fell below a statement of sympathetic interest, mine
would have to move upward in enthusiasm. This worked,
though it took a little time. Two days later the London *News
Chronicle,* reporting our statements, said: "The Foreign
Office adopted a warmer tone towards M. Schuman's plan
yesterday. Its first reaction, a few hours after the French
Foreign Minister's dramatic announcement, had been no-
ticeably cool."

But resentment still rankled. The next morning, arriving
at the room assigned to me in Lancaster House for our week
of meetings, I found word that Bevin had asked Schuman,
accompanied only by his interpreter, to join him in my room.

Schuman arrived solemn and puzzled; Bevin, gruff and
grumpy. He announced that he wanted to protest at the way
he had been treated. We were occupying Western Germany

jointly. This called for open and frank dealings between us, not secret deals. Now he was confronted with a *fait accompli* and he didn't like it at all. What he wanted to know was where he stood, what the rules were. And so on, getting more prickly as he talked. The interpreter was translating into Schuman's ear as Bevin spoke.

When he stopped, I asked to say something before Schuman replied. I told Schuman that I had not spoken to Bevin until Massigli's message, because I had promised to keep Schuman's plans confidential, and that I thought Bevin was convinced that my knowledge of the plan preceded his only because of my purely fortuitous decision to spend a day or two in Paris. I agreed that the first requirement of the grand alliance was full and frank disclosure and consultation between our three countries. I was sure Schuman must agree in this. Necessities growing out of domestic politics and methods of doing things sometimes warped the ideal. Only last September Mr. Bevin and Sir Stafford Cripps had been in Washington prior to the devaluation of the pound. They had discussed this impending event with us; but, although M. Schuman and M. Petsche, the French Minister of Finance, had also been in Washington, the exigencies of the situation had prevented similar discussions with them. Schuman and Petsche had, so far as I knew, never complained, although the devaluation affected them importantly. They had understood the unfortunate necessity of secrecy.

Bevin could stand it no longer: "Oh, hell," he said, "let's join the others. We're keepin' them waitin'." As we filed out of the room, Schuman squeezed my arm.

"My friend," he said, "you have a large deposit in my bank. You may draw on it whenever you please."

But Bevin had his revenge. Some days later at the end of a day I got a message to stop in his room in Lancaster House before going home.

"I know you like a Martini," said Ernie, "and it's hard to get a good one in London." Something was definitely afoot. I expressed guarded anticipation. At Bevin's signal, an ancient butler began operations at a sideboard. With growing disbelief I watched him pour into a tumbler one-third gin, one-third Italian vermouth, and one-third water without ice, then bring the tumbler to me on a tray.

Ernie was observing all this with what he thought was a Mona Lisa smile—but was more like the grin of a schoolboy up to deviltry.

It was clear that I could never drink this horror if I tasted it. The only course was to take it in one gulp, or call "uncle." I chose the former, and down it went.

"Have another," Ernie almost commanded.

"No, thank you," I said. "No one could make another just like that one."

It was not long before I was to need all the credit in Schuman's bank of which he had assured me. In my sketch of Ernest Bevin I have told of the proposal we made the following September for what General Bradley had described at the NATO meeting in May, 1950, as "balanced collective forces" for the defense of Europe, of our linking with that proposal another for the participation of German troops, and of the difficulties within the American government which delayed decision on these proposals until too late for adequate notice and preparation. I told also of our error in going ahead notwithstanding and of the adamant French opposition we encountered.

Day after day in that September of the Inchon landing, the debate went on in the Waldorf Tower, high above New York, first with the French and British, then within the NATO Council. Throughout it all, Schuman treated me with the greatest consideration and courtesy. Never using the ample material at hand for arguments *ad hominem,* never rattled by the increasing support we gained, as the days went by, from the other NATO Ministers, he remained cool, forceful, unyielding, but wholly detached. It was as though he were explaining a series of reactions in physics which had no relation to himself and which must occur in the way he stated, however much more pleasant and convenient it might be to have them take another course.

His agreement to our proposals would be quite meaningless, he said in private, since even if the government should support him, which it would not do, the Chamber would not support it. He understood our reasons for wanting German participation in European defense and, over time, thought them sound. But France was not ready for them at present. We had not thought the problem through, particularly the political setting essential to any German rearmament. He entirely recognized French obligation to do more than obstruct.

One afternoon, at the end of a meeting, Mr. Joseph Bech, the Foreign Minister of Luxembourg, a good friend, and one of the best-informed men in Europe, told me that things were not so dark as they looked, that Jean Monnet in Paris was working on a plan to bring the Germans into a military arrangement analogous to the Schuman Plan for coal and steel.

"Why doesn't Schuman tell me so?" I asked.

"Because he doesn't know it yet," he answered.

However that may have been, Hervé Alphand, who was with Schuman in New York, said to us, "Don't push Schuman so hard. He has to have time. We will work this out." And work it out they did over the ensuing months, first as the Pleven Plan and, the next year, as the European Defense Community. Nothing could have been more typical of Schuman's rare gifts than his ability to turn the necessity of opposition into an opportunity for constructive work.

As I have already recounted, General Marshall, who at

that moment happily became Secretary of Defense, agreed that we should cut our losses in this operation, and first try to obtain collective forces under unified command, leaving German participation to be agreed in principle, for the future. Some of my colleagues thought that the French suggestion of a possible supranational European defense organization was only a delaying tactic. But it made little difference, since there was no alternative.

These predictions, however, were quite wrong. Schuman went to work on the problem with the able help of Jean Monnet and Hervé Alphand. Soon a European working group was formed and not long afterward Ministers began to take tentative decisions. Closely as I followed their work, I was continually baffled by it until, during a long plane journey with Ambassador David Bruce, he gave me an understanding of the imaginative insight and political versatility of that gifted group. At the very moment when the Fourth Republic was demonstrating fatal defects as an instrument for directing the energies of Frenchmen in the national interest, this group was inventing new ways of directing the energies of Europeans in a new public interest broader than that of any nation—a European interest. Perhaps working in the confused and disordered politics of the Fourth Republic suggested to Schuman methods of approach to unity in Europe, which were hidden from me.

Certainly the obstacle which blocked my understanding of their work was an assumed need of orderliness and clarity. I approached the problem as would a lawyer member of one of our State constitutional conventions. A scheme of government should be logical and clear, and the whole should amount to sovereignty. But this was not true of Schuman's approach. Nor was it true of the drafters of our Constitution when they were working in Philadelphia. Even today, after nearly two centuries of interpretation by courts and by arms, the ambiguities they devised, attested to by many a five-to-four decision of the Supreme Court, leave room for maneuver.

Mr. G. M. Young's description of statesmen is supremely true of Robert Schuman: "Statesmen are not architects but gardeners working on such material as only nature can furnish, and . . . they never pull up a plant to see how the roots are doing."*

As one studies all the French-inspired postwar proposals looking toward the unification of Western Europe (Coal and Steel, Euratom, the Common Market, and EDC), one sees that the power—and very possibly the right—to secede remains in the various states. Even short of that, it is not always apparent how decisions of the organizations could be enforced against strong and determined dissidents. But it was the essence of the Schuman method not to attack the question of sovereignty head-on. Architecturally, the plans are defective and bewildering. But as living organisms rooted in the soil of European life, their very growth changes and modifies that life until they may become so entwined with and inseparable from it they may crack even masonry, as the roots of a tree will do. At such a time formal adjustments of sovereignty would seem merely ratification of the *status quo,* not changes from it.

In the summer of 1951, as the European Defense Community took form, my first impressions grew to a conviction that the United States should plump for this solution and do what could wisely be done to help it on. General Marshall agreed. Dispatches from Supreme Headquarters at Versailles showed General Eisenhower coming to the same conclusion. The President's approval made support of the EDC official U.S. policy.

This was progress, but a myriad of problems still hemmed us round—the level of forces needed (the existing military

---

* G. M. Young, *Stanley Baldwin* (Rupert Hart-Davis, London, 1952), p. 132.

estimates were vastly beyond any estimate of capability) and the source of the funds to equip and support them; the change of status of the allied forces in Germany from occupation forces, living by levies on the country, to members of a collective garrison collectively financed; the change of status of the West German government to accord with its new responsibilities. Added to all of these problems were others outside the German context—the working out of naval commands in the Mediterranean, North European waters, and the Atlantic, the wars in Korea and Indochina, the Iranian government's seizure of British oil properties, the Middle East and North Africa, and France's chronic state of international insolvency.

All in all, 1951 was not a quiet year. To add to its complexities, Great Britain spoke through three Foreign Ministers. Ernest Bevin resigned because of failing health in March. Herbert Morrison, who followed him, was a friend of many qualities and abilities, but none fitting him to deal with foreign affairs or foreigners. He was most knowledgeable about all that had to do with London and its government. He was an authentic House of Commons man. But he was unfamiliar with the problems to which he came. His departure with the political overturn of October, 1951, was, I have no doubt, welcome to him. Anthony Eden, who then took over, had had more experience in foreign affairs than any of us, but not in the postwar scene, a very different environment from any in which he had served, with the cold war mounting in intensity to the fury of the germ warfare accusations which the Chinese Communists made against us during the Korean War.

By September it was pretty plain that the specifications of the soldiers for European defense were too grandiose. So at Ottawa (in fact, its only accomplishment) the Three Wise Men, Averell Harriman, Jean Monnet, and Sir Edwin Plowden, Chairman of the U.K.'s Economic Planning Board, were appointed to reconcile plans with means. An attempt to solve the riddle of Mediterranean naval organization and command ended in the use of all the diplomacy of Schuman and Admiral Jerauld Wright of the U.S. delegation to keep peace between Morrison and the French Navy. The meeting despondently adjourned to convene two months later in Rome for another try.

As often happens, common troubles had brought Schuman and me even closer together. Our aims were the same and so were our views about the intractable material with which we had to work. We were in constant and private communication. The Rome meeting was another inconclusive one. The Three Wise Men reported; but German participation, still unresolved, prevented action. Tempers were fraying among our other Allies. In particular, my close and dear friend, Dirk Stikker, the Netherlands Foreign Minister, was disturbed lest the NATO Council be confronted with decisions in the making of which they had little part. That decisions of any sort would be made by anyone seemed to me most unlikely.

The Supreme Commander, General Eisenhower, spoke to us. I had never heard him in a large meeting before and found myself bewildered between the tone and the content of the speech. The tone was inspirational and vigorous; the content was the meagerest intellectual fare. To test the opinion of others, in the recess after the speech, I sought out my wise, shrewd, and humorous friend Mr. Joseph Bech, and asked him how he liked the speech.

"Ah," he said, "I think before long we shall lose our Supreme Commander." I was puzzled and doubtless showed it. "Yes," he went on, "the signs are unmistakable. Our Commander will soon leave us to run for President of your country." And so he did, less than four months later.

Rome, like Ottawa, adjourned to try again, this time at Lisbon in February, 1952. Lisbon, it seemed to me, would be the last clear chance. Time was running out. For a year and a half we seemed to have made no progress toward a defense of Europe or toward European unification. But, in fact, we had. The very running of time had adjusted attitudes, and all the while the EDC was coming closer to formulation and ministerial agreement. Nonetheless, if the tide did not turn at Lisbon, it would turn, if at all, too late for the aims toward which Schuman and I were working. France's troubles were mounting in Indochina and North Africa; the Fourth Republic was showing less, rather than more, capacity to deal with its problems; Schuman's own position in the French political scene was not improving; and the Truman administration was entering what could well be its last year. It was with these thoughts that we went to Lisbon after preparatory meetings in London with the French, British, and Germans.

The meetings in London dealt chiefly with preparations for German participation: the agreements as to what arms could and could not be made in Germany, what aircraft, how much Germany should pay for the support of allied troops on her soil pending the development of her own contribution. We made progress, but haltingly. More often than not, I found myself agreeing with positions taken by Adenauer; and Eden, with Schuman. It would not do to allow a split to develop. One of the tasks of Lisbon would be to work out a united allied position which the Germans could find reasonable.

The Lisbon Council meeting got off to a good start with a day of glorious sunshine, a most welcome change from the rain and fog of London. In his opening speech the Portuguese Foreign Minister, Dr. Paulo da Cunha, spoke of having arranged the weather as a welcome for us. Following him, I referred enviously to the scope and power of the Foreign

Office in Portugal. Eden, coming after me, added that he wished it clearly understood that in England responsibility for the weather rested wholly on the Home Office.

Our week of NATO meetings at Lisbon was interspersed with meetings with the British and French, and with the French alone. The French group was made up of Premier Edgar Faure, Schuman, and Bidault, who was Minister of Defense. Faure impressed me by his youth, his competence, and the extent of his knowledge of the problems. He had been in office only a short time and expected to remain there only a few weeks more. But he was confident, decisive, and very good. Bidault impressed me as indecisive and confused, sometimes to the point of being incomprehensible to me. After a day or two he fell ill and went home. A deputy took his place.

The American team consisted of Robert Lovett, Secretary of Defense, John Snyder, Secretary of the Treasury, Averell Harriman, Mutual Security Administrator, and myself. We worked together happily and effectively. What was done at Lisbon would have been impossible if they had not been present there with me, participating in the same meetings, subject to the same pressures, reaching the same judgments. For difficult action was required by all their Departments; and man's inhumanity to man is never revealed more starkly than by one colleague to another far away at the end of a cable line pleading for help with a fervor which in Washington always seems hysterical. As it was, even joining as the others did in the recommendations which we sent to the President, we had to ask his intervention to tell their Departments to stop arguing and do what he had approved. Authority fades with distance and with the speed of light.

The key to success at Lisbon lay with the French and necessitated solution of the German arms production dispute and of financial problems which the Wise Men's military program would present to France. The other member nations were ready to accept the recommendations of the Wise Men; the British, the Germans, and ourselves had worked out all our differences. Everything centered on the French, with the Germans and ourselves the only visible sources of help.

Our talks took on a nightmarish quality when they entered the maze of the French budget. Concealed in it were differing judgments of the cost of the war in Indochina, alleged military production, which was in reality unemployment relief, and obsolete munitions plants kept operating because closing them would be embarrassing if the Germans were to begin production. But, however we looked at it, there remained a gap between the needs and the means available in the budget.

On the last afternoon agreement was reached between French defense and treasury people and ours that the gap should be filled by an increase in French resources allocated to defense, by increased German contribution to support of French troops in Germany, and by increased U.S. aid. The balance of payments gap—the dollar gap—was to be filled by procurement orders placed in France and a stepping-up of U.S. airfield construction and NATO supply lines. The whole operation was like one of those games where a dozen little shots have to be maneuvered into holes in a cardboard field; the slightest jar in trying to get the last one in shakes all the others out.

At ten o'clock the last evening of the Lisbon session, the French, the British, and ourselves met in the British Embassy to receive the report of the working committee, to approve it (*Deo volente*), and to prepare a joint message urging upon Adenauer a valiant effort to meet the quota asked of the Germans. I had already prepared my own personal message to him saying, "This is it," and explaining that it was now or never so far as German participation in defense was concerned. Schuman had not worked through the financial sessions and did not understand the significance of the figures. It took about an hour to go through them. Schuman was tired; Eden was catching a cold; time was getting short. As the mathematics class wore on, Schuman yawned, Eden sneezed, and I became fidgety.

A little before midnight agreement was reached and the working group, jointly instructed by the three of us, retired to the dining room to work. Schuman, pleading weariness, went to the French Embassy. Eden and I sought refreshment while we waited for the papers.

In half an hour the group reappeared, deadlocked over a matter on which the French had understood the instructions differently from the British and Americans. Eden and I argued with them, but they were adamant. They could not take the responsibility of accepting our view, nor would they call Schuman. He had gone home to bed and could not be disturbed. Nothing more could be done that night. Then I got my first experience of the famous Eden temper. He simply exploded. His fury was impressive and effective. I remember one sentence which went something like this: "Every time a crisis occurs in the world some damned Frenchman goes to bed." He told the French staff that, if they didn't straighten this out with Schuman on the telephone, he would go to their Embassy and get it straight himself.

This did it. A sleepy and puzzled Schuman confirmed the instructions as we understood them, and told his people that, if they had any further doubts, they were to take instructions from me. Shortly after this Eden announced that he had to go to bed. I said, "Well, I suppose I could say that in every crisis some damned Englishman goes to bed." This obtained from him a similar instruction to the British group. Until four o'clock that morning, when the papers were finished, approved, and dispatched by special plane to Bonn, Atlantic union was pretty much personified by me in the drawing room of the British Embassy in Lisbon.

Later in the morning Adenauer and the High Commissioners reached agreement in Bonn, and the Lisbon meeting ended in a glow of agreement, good will, and optimism. The next step would be working out the innumerable details of ending the occupation, amending the North Atlantic Treaty to permit German association, and bringing the EDC to finality and signature. We set our sights to do this by the following May. But, before it was done, Schuman, Eden, and I were to have another all-night session, this time in Bonn.

The High Commissioners and their staffs had done a vast amount of work with the Germans, putting aside, however, the most controversial points—not only with the Germans but among the Allies—for the Foreign Ministers. We arrived at Bonn on May 23, 1952. I stayed with the McCloys in their delightful house on a bluff overlooking the Rhine, with its unbelievable activity. Barges pass unendingly in both directions. Flying every flag in Europe, the processions went on from dawn to dark, when they drew out of the channel and anchored. Watching the spectacle was habit-forming; one could stop only by getting out of sight of it.

Schuman, while as courteous and alert as ever, was unusually quiet and worried. He told us that he was not at all sure that he had the Cabinet with him. One of the principal concerns of the French was over some form of guarantee from the United States and Britain that the Germans, once in the EDC with armed divisions of German troops, would not withdraw from it and go off on an independent course.

Before we went to Bonn, this matter had been carefully studied in the Department and reviewed with the President. He had already announced that he would not again be a candidate for the Presidency, and believed that it would be unwise to attempt any development of foreign policy which appeared to be novel. What we did should have its roots in policy already approved by Congress. We, therefore, worked out a formula to the effect that the United States was deeply concerned as a matter of security, not only with NATO, but with EDC, since they were bound together and anything which affected the unity or integrity of either of these organizations would be regarded as a threat to the security of the United States and dealt with under the North Atlantic Treaty.

All of Friday afternoon and night until three or four o'clock Saturday morning was devoted, in large part, to this problem. I put forward our proposal. Eden picked it up and did very well with it, pointing out that it went further in meeting French concern than he had thought possible and offering to join in it, as Britain later did. Schuman should urge the Cabinet to regard the proposal as a great concession to France rather than to find flaws in it. Schuman kept sending telegrams to Paris and making telephone calls. The replies dispirited him. He was so tired that he would doze off while he was waiting for replies to his messages. Eden, McCloy, and I would use these intervals to improve the language of our proposal in an effort to meet worries in Paris.

Our meeting with Adenauer and his staff, set for ten o'clock Saturday morning, had to be put off until two o'clock, then till four, to gain more time for Schuman. When we did start in, the French position on some questions was undecided and remained so for another twenty-four hours. So confused did the exchange become that at one time Paris asked for a change which was actually less favorable to France than the proposal offered. Eden and I started to point this out to Schuman and then decided that for him to argue this with Paris would only complicate his problem. So we accepted the amendment without comment.

The next week, after some signing ceremonies in Bonn,

we went on to Paris for the final and larger ceremony involving all the NATO nations. There I had an experience which showed me the depth and nature of Schuman's difficulties.

The President of France, who with Mme. Auriol had always been very kind to my wife and me, asked our Ambassador to bring me to see him privately. We went to the Élysée Palace expecting to make a social call. The President received us alone in his own study. He told us with considerable passion that our policy toward Germany was a great mistake. He knew Germany; he reviewed German history since Bismarck. We were wrong in thinking that the greater danger came from Russia. It came from Germany.

I asked what alternative he suggested. He urged the original postwar policy of the four powers controlling Germany. When we pointed out that that had been tried and that the only Soviet agreement obtainable was one which would put all Germany under Soviet control, he did not agree. We parted gloomily, but I had a better understanding of what Schuman was up against.

I have often wondered whether the accident of the calendar, that the American election came in 1952 rather than in 1953, may not have had a profound effect on the history of Europe and upon Schuman's place in that history. The Lisbon decisions, their translation into formal agreements regarding Germany and NATO in May, and the prompt ratification by Congress of our undertakings and of the Japanese Peace Treaty had generated great momentum toward institutions to unify, and thereby strengthen, the direction of defense, economic, and political affairs in Europe.

But as the summer wore on and the American presidential campaign began, it was clear that the dynamo had stopped. At first the full significance of President Truman's announcement that he would not be a candidate for re-election was not apparent to Europe. But, as the conventions made their nominations, Europe became aware that whatever the result of the election no one who had been speaking and deciding for the United States would be doing either after January, 1953. So governments waited to see with whom they would deal. The puzzlement grew, as Mr. Stevenson said what Europe had expected to hear from its late Supreme Commander, and heard from him what it had expected to hear from Senator Taft.

The momentum of the spring and early summer died. Europe still waited. Nothing visible happened; but decay and disintegration set in. Second thoughts took the place of earlier thoughts. A man who looked like a man of destiny, but wasn't, Premier Mendès-France, regarded EDC with a cold, if not hostile, eye. After the new American administration took office, it required time to take hold, and also it was not at all clear who was going to furnish American leadership —Mr. Dulles and the State Department or Senator McCarthy and Messrs. Cohn and Schine. The President cut the military budget by $5 billion.

The momentum and movement of the first half of 1952 were not recovered again, or American leadership re-established. On August 30, 1954, the French Chamber killed EDC, despite Mr. Dulles's threats of "agonizing reappraisal" of our foreign policy which must take place should EDC fail.

Fate was unkind to Robert Schuman. Another year of energetic pushing and close relations among Washington, London, and the continent, given the strong forward thrust of May, 1952, might have put EDC into effect and brought about the conference on political unification scheduled to meet six months after its ratification. This might have happened. It is not a fantastic possibility. If it had happened, is there a Frenchman of this century who would have ranked with Schuman? Clemenceau? Possibly. De Gaulle? But De Gaulle might not have had his second chance.

Of course, it can be argued that, if the momentum of the spring of 1952 had resulted in ratification of EDC, it would have been only formal and that the seeds of retreat had already germinated and were bound to flower. While it is true that reaction from the unremitting effort of the past twelve years would certainly have come, it need not have wiped out the consequences of a ratification of EDC. As Jean Monnet has wisely said, the thinking of people is conditioned and confined by the frame within which it takes place. Once a small, restricting frame is broken and thought expands into a wider setting, the effect is most unlikely to be undone. The rate of change can be slowed, but the mold once broken cannot be used again. EDC, and perhaps the beginning of the political community of Europe, would not have been impossible if pressure had been maintained for another year, and it could have affected profoundly all that followed in the decade of the fifties. But it is enough to suggest the might-have-been without pushing it too hard.

In honesty, one must concede that between this glimmering dream and reality stood not only the paralysis of the American election but a hampering trait in Schuman's own nature. One of the topics on which he discoursed a good deal and obviously thought much about was "French public opinion." He spoke of it always as a potent but unreasonable, even whimsical, sovereign, which would not permit this or that. "Public opinion" never seemed to want anything positive, except financial support and endorsement of French policies in Indochina and North Africa. None of Schuman's inventiveness seemed directed toward ways of influencing "public opinion" directly. In time, it would come to accept meritorious ideas, but one did not do anything to aid in the process, other than maneuver and speak in the Chamber of Deputies. He and Sam Rayburn seemed to me to look at the problem of public opinion in the same way.

When he was struggling hard to get the Chamber to accept the EDC, I talked with him about the organization built by the Citizens Committee for the Marshall Plan in 1947 and 1948, and the prodigious effort made to reach leaders and groups at the grass roots, before pounding the corridors of the Senate and House Office Buildings.

He listened, as though I were a modern Marco Polo, as I outlined the crisscrossed form of organized persuasion, by geographical groups, to concentrate on congressional and senatorial constituencies, supplemented by interest organizations, such as foreign policy associations, church groups, women's clubs, labor unions, chambers of commerce, the innumerable groups of the "knife and fork" circuit—the Rotary, Kiwanis, and other clubs. Perhaps most puzzling of all to him was the bipartisan nature of these efforts and why official party decisions were not necessary to bring about association of their members in an effort like the Marshall Plan or the Reciprocal Trade Agreements program, etc.

It would not work in France, he felt sure of that—more sure than I did, observing what General de Gaulle could do when he tried. Our political parties are, to be sure, public parties rather than members' parties—that is, run to gather public and nonmember votes rather than to express with precision the views of the members, and to split into subparties when the members differ on the true faith. So, with us, if important groups warmly accept an idea, the parties can be expected to endorse it, rather than *vice versa*.

But Schuman never had or created, or perhaps never could create, the organization to propagandize at the grass roots for EDC. This, I believe, was one of its principal weaknesses and one of the reasons for its ultimate failure. Not since that golden age of politics in England, before the Reform Bill of 1867 had really begun to make universal suffrage effective, has political leadership been able to rest with good ideas and brilliant debate in the legislative body. As Robert Lowe, Viscount Sherbrooke, said when the Reform Bill was passed, "We must educate our masters." I wonder whether one of the basic defects of the Fourth Republic was the impossibility of discovering under its procedures who they were and then educating them.

In November, 1952, our masters in the United States decided unmistakably that they wanted a change in the directing personnel and, less certainly, in the policies of the United States government. In the following month the French Chamber overthrew the Pinay government and ended Schuman's tenure at the Quai d'Orsay. In response to a note from me of farewell and affection, I received a letter, in longhand and in English, so typical of this gallant and gentle and great man that, with his permission, I cannot do better than close this sketch with his own words, written March 5, 1953:

> Dear Mr. Acheson:
>
> I answer your letter last of all, after completing my resettlement in a more normal life. For I wanted to meditate upon it as upon a message of your friendship and the review of what has been achieved during four heavily loaded years.
>
> I have always kept in mind the words you had spoken to me one day, in the presence of our late colleague Bevin: "France must have the leadership for Europe." This was for me a programme and a personal responsibility. It also meant the establishment between us of a mutual reliance which never failed, even during the most difficult debates. When we exchanged messages or trusted each other with some confidence, we knew we expressed ourselves with total conviction and frankness.

I owe you for this a particular gratitude; such a feeling of secureness in diplomatic relations is exceptional.

Fate decided that we would finish our task together, at the same moment, when a new stage is about to begin for our two countries. In spite of the doubts and of disputes which arise in France on the eve of serious but unescapable decisions, I am confident that reason will finally prevail. What has been created cannot be repudiated any more, and no other policy could win over a majority, be it only an occasional one.

I do my best to support the present government in its continuation of a policy which has been mine and which, let us hope it be without any drawbacks, allows of a certain new stress and of slight differences, which seem however acceptable. It was necessary not to complicate the situation with personal difficulties.

I am very much impressed by the growing audience our ideas find in France and beyond our frontiers, especially among the young. The freedom which has been given back to me offers me the opportunity to work efficiently to serve these ideas.

My political activity has become parliamentary instead of being governmental; neither its orientation nor its briskness have changed. Yours has suffered an eclipse, which I deeply regret.

But you are one of those men who can withdraw, but whom neither their country nor their friends can forget. You have left a deep mark in my life, as well as in the history of my country, of Europe and of the world. Let us thank you for this achievement.

I add to these feelings of gratefulness my thanks to Mrs. Acheson who has always been so kind and friendly to me.

Very faithfully yours,
Robert Schuman

III

WINSTON SPENCER CHURCHILL[*]

British Prime Minister, 1940–1945, 1951–1955

Early one morning during the war I was summoned to the White House from my office across the street in the old State Department, where I was an Assistant Secretary dealing with economic matters. Harry Hopkins received me in the Lincoln bedroom and in the Lincoln bed—that is, he was in the bed. He wanted some information and he wanted it quickly.

At the time Mr. Churchill was staying in the White House. Indeed, that was the cause of the summons. The President's strong competitive instinct, Harry explained to me, led him to try to keep up with Mr. Churchill in everything. But in one contest he was definitely outclassed, as became evident as the after-dinner hours passed. Sometimes during these evenings the Prime Minister would produce a slip of paper and suggest that he and President Roosevelt initial conclusions reached earlier in the day. On these occasions Harry would pocket the memorandum for more mature consideration.

He had such a paper that morning, and wanted the facts on a point falling within my official field. As we discussed the matter, the bedroom door opened and in walked the author of the memorandum in pajamas and bathrobe, smoking a

---

[*] Mr. Churchill was made a knight of the Most Noble Order of the Garter in April, 1953. He is referred to in this sketch by his titles during the period which it covers.

cigar. (There is no such thing, I submit, as a good after-breakfast cigar.) I was presented and shortly withdrew. Even in pajamas the aura of command hung about him. The bathrobe could no more disguise his eminence than the toga could Caesar's.

In March, 1946, Lord and Lady Halifax asked my wife and me to lunch at the British Embassy with the recent speaker at Fulton, Missouri, and his daughter Sarah. The town was still rocking with that famous "iron curtain" speech. Congress was in an uproar. The British loan agreement was supposed to be threatened, and the British government in the next month thought it wise, on the inquiry of Congressman Louis Ludlow, to disassociate itself from the speech. Later, during his same visit to this country, I offended Mr. Churchill, to my great regret, by not attending a dinner for him in New York upon the advice of my Department colleagues. But that day he could not have been more agreeable. This was largely due to my wife. Mr. Churchill had no more devoted admirer. Moreover, she told him so with expositive detail. This treatment is almost certain to produce a benign effect upon the hearer, as it did in this instance. The great man was in no hurry to terminate "such dulcet and harmonious breath," but, in time, he felt that turn about was fair play and made inquiry into the interests of his pleasant and perspicacious luncheon partner. He discovered that she was a painter, another bond. She had seen reproductions of his pictures and praised them honestly and warmly. Expansively he said, with no suspicion that the ground onto which he ventured was mined:

"You can help me. Give me a criticism." He would not be put off. In statesmanship the lady's interest was that of a spectator and amateur; but in painting she was a performer and a professional. Standards of honesty are more exacting in the latter role.

"Very well," she said. "Your palette is keyed too high. Your work would have more depth if it were toned down."

"You are quite wrong," Mr. Churchill broke in. "My palette is based on advice by most eminent painters," naming some. The lady pointed out that the question was one of judgment and not of fact, and that her judgment was not affected by authority. She went on to point out specific instances where in her view a lowering of tone would have brought improvement. He fought back with spirit. Neither gave ground nor asked for quarter.

As we got up from the table, his cigar was going like a steam locomotive on a stiff grade. "A woman of conviction, your wife," he said to me. After that she was a favorite of his. The Churchills could not have been kinder to us, asking us to their house, often for lunch alone with them, both when they were in office and out of it.

At one of these luncheons at No. 10 Downing Street Anthony Eden was also a guest. We lunched in the small apartment on the top floor, formerly servants' quarters, which had been done over for family use in the days of austerity when the state rooms were closed. While we were having sherry, the Prime Minister took Eden and me over to the sitting room windows overlooking the small garden and, beyond the garden wall, the Horse Guards Parade. He kept poking me in the ribs to indicate that mischief was afoot.

"Give me your advice," he said. "You see how those plane trees along the garden wall interfere with the view from here of the parade ground. They spoil an otherwise perfect spot to see the Trooping of the Colour. I'm thinking of having them taken away. What do you say?"

"My God, Winston," Eden exploded, "you can't do that. You don't own the place." Churchill gave me another delighted poke. "Who's to stop me?" he rumbled. "What are you so excited about? I live here, don't I?"

"That's just it," said Eden, walking into the trap. "You only live here. You don't own it. It's just plain vandalism to cut down those trees."

"Ah, I see!" A great light seemed to dawn on Churchill, as he gave me one last nudge. "I only live here, the life tenant, so to speak, and you inherit the place. What do they call you? —The remainderman, that's it." He walked off chuckling.

"The old boy got me that time," said Eden, as we followed him in to luncheon.

Churchill always had his own bottle of champagne by his place at the table, to be independent of the vagaries of butlers, Mrs. Churchill would explain. They seemed fated to pass it when his glass was full and never when he wanted it.

One evening at dinner on the President's yacht, *Williamsburg,* discussion of champagne and related joys led Churchill to an interesting experiment. Lord Cherwell, formerly Professor Lindemann of Oxford and an intimate of the Prime Minister's, was in the company. He was known as "Prof."

"Prof, have you got your slide rule?" asked Churchill. The question was unnecessary as Lord Cherwell always carried one and instantly produced it. Talk around the table stopped as everyone waited to see what was about to happen. Churchill asked the President the dimensions of the *Williamsburg's* dining saloon and got them. He had been thinking, he said, as he sat at dinner that from the age of sixteen to that evening, about sixty-two years, he had consumed on the average about a quart of wines and spirits a day, sometimes none, when none was available, sometimes more; but on the average about a quart. As he looked about him, a question rose in his mind and would give him no peace until he knew the answer. If all those wines and spirits were poured into this saloon, how deep would they be?

The "Prof's" slide rule flew back and forth as he made the

The Senate Foreign Relations Committee opens hearings on NATO, April, 1949. The author and Senators Alexander Smith, Alexander Wiley, Arthur Vandenberg, and Tom Connally. (UPI)

The author and Foreign Ministers Vyshinsky, Schuman, and Bevin at the Quai d'Orsay, May, 1949. (UPI)

Cartoon by Cabral from *Franc-Tireur,* Paris, May 21-22, 1949, entitled *"Les Trois."* (L. to R.) Andrei Vyshinsky, Robert Schuman, Ernest Bevin, the author.

The Grand Salon of the Palais Rose being prepared for the Conference of Foreign Ministers, May, 1949. (UPI)

In the lift of the Quai d'Orsay: Ernest Bevin, the author, an attendant, Robert Schuman, May, 1949. (UPI)

Konrad Adenauer in September, 1949. (WIDE WORLD)

The author and Governor Thomas E. Dewey at a Mayor's dinner for the United Nations Chief of Mission, New York. (PHOTOGRAPHED AT THE WALDORF ASTORIA)

'They're Playing Their Cards A Little Cautiously, Now—'

Cartoon in the Washington *Post*, May, 1949, by kind permission of Herblock.

The author and British Foreign Minister Anthony Eden conferring at the General Assembly of the United Nations in Paris, November, 1951.

At the Pentagon, October, 1950, discussing a unified defense of Europe: M. Jules Moch, French Minister of Defense; Secretary of Defense George C. Marshall; the author.

Aboard the Presidential yacht *Williamsburg:* Prime Minister Churchill and President Truman before a painting of the engagement between the U.S.S. *Constitution* and H.M.S. *Java.*

Prime Minister Antonio de Oliveira Salazar of Portugal and a head from the *"Painel dos pescadores"* by Nuno Gonçalves (*circa* 1465) in the Museu das Janelas Verdes, Lisbon.

The receiving line at a state dinner for the British Prime Minister at Anderson House, Washington, January, 1952: Mr. Churchill, Mrs. Acheson, and the author. (UPI)

At the Pentagon in January, 1952. Seated, l. to r.: the author; Prime Minister Churchill; Secretary of Defense Lovett; Foreign Minister Eden. Standing, Admiral Sir Roderick R. McGrigor, First Sea Lord; The Honorable W. Averell Harriman; Field Marshal Sir William Slim, Chief of the Imperial General Staff; Sir Oliver Franks, British Ambassador; and General of the Army Omar N. Bradley.

Children from the Vienna Ballet School, dancing in the Ballhausplatz, June 30, 1952.

The stage of the theater in the Hofburg during the performance of *The Marriage of Figaro,* June 29, 1952.

computations. We waited eagerly. In no time at all he was ready. "Well?" urged Churchill.

"Just under two and a half feet," announced Cherwell. Churchill shook his head sadly.

As I wrote to Mike Pearson of Canada a few days later, "The results were very disappointing to the Old Man. He had expected that we would all be swimming like goldfish in a bowl, whereas it would hardly come up to our knees."

During the visit at which this dinner took place, the first after Sir Winston's return to power in the winter of 1951–52, the issue of the Atlantic command under NATO precipitated the most dramatic meeting which I can remember. Under the Attlee government, Parliament had accepted the principle that the Atlantic command—as distinct from the Channel command and that of the Western approaches to Great Britain—should be American. The predominance of American naval power left no other practical possibility. But Churchill, when in opposition, had spoken against it. One of the tasks of his visit was to translate the prior agreement into an operating command. Churchill, despite a number of extensions of the British commands, still refused agreement. Decision was deferred until he made a visit to Canada.

The critical meeting was set for the afternoon after his return. A most spectacular briefing was arranged at the Pentagon for the morning; a long rest provided after lunch. But, as the Americans waited in the Cabinet Room for the President and the Prime Minister, the British came in badly shaken. They had met Churchill in the President's anteroom to show him a new draft of agreement on the American command. He had read it, torn it up, and marched into the President's office without a word. The First Sea Lord, a little Scotsman, Admiral Sir Rhoderick Robert McGrigor, summed up the situation. "Hurricane warnings along the Potomac!"

he said. At that the two heads of government entered and we took our seats, the British on one side of the Cabinet table, the Americans on the other.

The President opened the meeting in his brusque way. We were resuming consideration of the Atlantic command; he had nothing to add to what he had said before; had the Prime Minister any comments? We then listened to what I think was the most eloquent and moving speech I have ever heard. It was simplicity itself. For centuries England had kept alight the flame of freedom, fighting every tyrant who would have put it out, and carrying the flame over every sea to all the continents. The major burden now, the primacy, had passed to us. But Britain could and would still do her part, and she asked to do it, a right she had earned, in that element which was peculiarly hers, upon the sea (I can remember some of his words), "upon that Western sea whose floor is white with the bones of Englishmen." Here Britain, wresting the command from Spain and then from France, used it to put teeth in our defiance of European penetration of our hemisphere. In the plenitude of our power and responsibility there was surely room for generosity in sharing the burden of responsibility. The awful burden of atomic power and command was ours. Here lay the final word of peace or war. Must we still ask that Britain waive its historic place on that small and daily shrinking sea?

Thus, in outline, the speech took its majestic course. As it progressed, Sir Oliver Franks, the British Ambassador, passed a note to me across the table. It read, "Be very, very careful." I listened even more carefully, trying to catch something beyond the beauty of rhetoric. It seemed to me that I did. In any event, Franks's message was clear warning that this was no time for a matter-of-fact reply and pressure for a decision.

Sitting on the President's right, I whispered a request to be allowed to speak when the Prime Minister finished. He nodded. No one who wished to make an impression would have asked for the assignment of following that speech of Winston Churchill's. My purpose was threefold: to get the floor and hold it preclusively; to allow the almost unbearable tension to relax; and to probe. So it was a rambling effort as I felt around. After an obvious opening, I sympathized with Mr. Churchill in being asked to agree to the American command. It was not his idea; he had been opposed to it, and publicly opposed. The Prime Minister began to listen attentively and to nod his head. I dared not look toward the President or Bob Lovett, who were wondering what was going on. Then very cautiously I tried another tack. How often all of us had found ourselves accepting a course of action which was far from what it should be, in order to get on with a job. Most things had a way of looking pretty muddled by the time a lot of people had tinkered with them. Again he showed interested approval.

This was enough. I suggested that the President might wish to recess the meeting for a few minutes, while a few of us went into his office to bring in a suggestion. Churchill seconded the idea.

As I recall it, the group included Oliver Franks, Admiral McGrigor, and Air Chief Marshal Sir William Elliot from one side of the table, Secretary of Defense Robert Lovett, Admiral William Fechteler, Chief of Naval Operations, and General Omar Bradley, Chairman of the Joint Chiefs of Staff, from the other. As we closed the door, Bill Fechteler burst out, "How long are we going to fool around with his damned talk?"

"Forget it, Bill," said Lovett. "Dean has got something in mind; but what it is I couldn't guess."

"I think it's the answer," contributed Franks.

My guess was that we had all come close to bungling the whole business. We had been trying to persuade the P.M.

to agree to the American Atlantic command. This called for
reversal of a position he had publicly taken, which he would
never do. The harder he was pressed, the more stubbornly
he would resist. But it was quite unnecessary for him to
agree. His Majesty's Government had already agreed. The
real question was whether he wished to stop defense measures
already in process of execution. The answer to that was
clearly that he did not. The Prime Minister could, at the
same time, maintain his own opinion and loyally further any
and all actions for the common defense which the two governments had undertaken.

"I don't get it," said Admiral Fechteler. "Does he agree or
doesn't he? We've got to get that settled."

"Bill," said General Bradley, "if you will just take it easy,
I think the answer for your purposes is yes."

While we waited for a dictated communiqué to be typed,
a message from the President urged haste. We filed back into
the room as the last sheet came off the machine and with
Oliver Franks's final instruction, "You read it, Dean, and no
one else says anything."

The President, the Prime Minister, and I had the only
copies. I read the short statement slowly. It began by referring to "arrangements about the Atlantic Command recom-
mended by NATO and accepted by the late Government of
the United Kingdom," and to alterations "to extend the
United Kingdom home command to the 100 fathom line."
Then came the heart of the matter: "These changes however do not go the full way to meet the Prime Minister's
objections to the original arrangements. Nevertheless, the
Prime Minister, while not withdrawing his objections, expressed his readiness to allow the appointment of a Supreme
Commander to go forward in order that a command structure may be created and enabled to proceed with the necessary planning in the Atlantic area. He reserved the right to

bring forward modifications for the consideration of NATO, if he so desired, at a later stage."

The moment of silence which followed began to be unendurable. Then Churchill brought his hand down with a slam on the paper. "I accept every word of it," he said.

"I, too," said the President; then to a secretary behind him, "Have this run off and given out at once."

"Shall we have the two press secretaries review it for language, Mr. President?" he was asked.

"I don't think so," said the President. "The Prime Minister and I have both been over it, and one of us, at least, uses fair English."

Not long after this visit King George VI died, in February, 1952. President Truman appointed me his Special Ambassador to represent him at the funeral. Immediately after there was to be a four-power meeting (Great Britain, France, Germany, and the United States) in London, followed by a NATO meeting in Lisbon, to get on with German participation in a defense force for Europe. Two years before at luncheon in Buckingham Palace, the King had spoken in great appreciation of Mr. Churchill's meticulous consideration in keeping him informed of every aspect of the war and in consulting with him fully on its every turn. I marveled then at the capacity of this extraordinary man to perform duties of so wide a scope without ever seeming hurried or harassed.

This talk came back to me when sending the official message of condolence. So I sent Mr. Churchill a private message referring to the close bond which I knew had existed between him and the Monarch and expressing sympathy for the deep personal sorrow which his death had brought to the Prime Minister. Waiting for me on my arrival in London was an invitation to lunch with the Churchills. He was moved by my message and spoke through lunch of the late King with the same affectionate respect and admiration with which the King had spoken of him.

"How will it be now?" I asked. "The Queen is a very young woman. Will you tell her the sort of somber and intricate matters you discussed with her father? And will she listen?"

"Of course I will," he answered. "She is the Monarch; my duty is the same. And," he added, "I think she will listen. She has a good head."

This talk was to have consequences which might have gotten me into trouble with Anthony Eden if he had not been good-natured about it.

The London four-power meetings, as I have described in my sketch of Robert Schuman, raised some difficult questions, to all of which answers were not found in London. On some of these I found myself more in agreement with Adenauer than with Eden and Schuman. On the last day of the session Queen Elizabeth received the French Foreign Minister M. Schuman, Chancellor Adenauer, and me. I went to Clarence House, the first of the three. The Queen, accompanied by Eden and the Duke of Edinburgh, received me in a small drawing room. As Her Majesty motioned us to our chairs, she regretted the weather, which was typical for London in February, and hoped that our meetings had gone well. Hesitating over a formal answer to her question which would say nothing, I remembered my conversation of a few days earlier and was tempted into more than a conversational minuet.

So I answered that the meetings had gone only fairly well, reported the tendency to divide, and explained why this was bothersome. Eden looked pained; the Queen and the Duke, interested. The Queen asked me to illustrate, which I did, picking an issue on which we and the Germans had a particularly good case, and taking care not to weaken it. The Duke wondered whether Eden would like to add anything.

He did; but his annoyance at me somewhat deflected his aim. There was no doubt now that our hosts were enjoying the talk. They egged me on and waived aside the announcement that M. Schuman had arrived and was waiting.

I began to regret my innovation in audiences with constitutional sovereigns, but, once started, could not turn back. It was some relief to me when, upon another announcement of M. Schuman's patient presence, the Queen's rising ended what she kindly said was a most interesting talk.

That evening, after our flight to Portugal, Eden was dining with us at the Embassy in Lisbon. When he arrived, he said, "I don't know why I speak to you. You behaved very badly this afternoon."

"Did Her Majesty say that?" I asked.

"You know very well she didn't," he answered. "That was the trouble. You did it with malice aforethought." I pleaded Churchill in extenuation and was finally forgiven under the benign influence of the Ambassador's Martinis.

During that same visit to London, I had my most strenuous encounter with the Prime Minister. It came out of an unclouded sky. Ambassador Gifford and I had dined on that last evening in London, before going to Lisbon, at the Foreign Minister's official residence with our British, French, and German colleagues. We spent a good many hours after dinner trying to reduce the remaining points of disagreement among us. It was well after midnight when we returned to the old Embassy at No. 14 Prince's Gate. Epps, the Embassy's incomparable butler, was waiting up for us. He handed me a fat sealed envelope with "No. 10 Downing Street" on the outside.

"This came for you less than an hour ago," he said. I decided to take it upstairs to look at in the morning, said goodnight, and went off to bed. Everything on our floor was dark and silent. My wife was asleep. From the room of Luke Battle,

my assistant, came the unmistakable sound of a good con-
science. I got ready to turn in. Ought I to look into that
wretched envelope? I knew of nothing important pending
with the Prime Minister. And yet, why should he send a
paper in the middle of the night? The chances for sleep were
dim either way—whether I left it alone and worried about
it, or opened it and thought about the contents. So I broke
the seal, and in a moment knew that there was to be no sleep
for me that night.

The letter said only that, as I knew, the Prime Minister
would be speaking in a few days in the House on a motion
put down by the Opposition. He had dictated what he proposed to say. He thought that it posed no problems and,
unless he heard from me to the contrary, would take it that
I saw none. A glance through the speech revealed a problem
of considerable dimensions.

Regretfully I woke Luke Battle. When, with the aid of
cold water, he was fully conscious, he got Epps to have some
coffee made, and telephoned the hotels where my secretary,
Miss Barbara Evans, and Mr. Paul Nitze of the State Department's Policy Planning Staff were staying to wake them
and ask them to come to the Embassy at once. The Marine
Guard at the Embassy Chancery was told to alert the night
stenographic staff.

The motion to which the Prime Minister's speech was
directed criticized him personally for sins of commission or
omission, I forget which, having the result, in the opinion
of the Opposition, of encouraging the United States to expand the area of hostilities in Korea. The motion would be
defeated; but some Conservative leaders were not inclined to
overexert themselves in the Prime Minister's defense, upon
the unhappy theory that "ill blows the wind that profits no-
body."

Churchill's draft speech did not merely answer his critics;

it slew them. It stated exactly what action his critics, when in power, had agreed with us should be taken, if, after General MacArthur's defeat in North Korea, worst came to worst. These orders were top secret, and, perhaps, still are. At any rate it was out of the question that their specific contents should be revealed. It was enough for the Prime Minister's purpose to state that his critics had agreed to measures which went beyond those for which they criticized him. They would know what they had agreed to.

By three o'clock my sleepy coadjutors had assembled. The papers I showed them and hot coffee woke them up. We had two jobs to do. One was to write a letter saying that under no circumstances should the instructions referred to be revealed; that no one short of the President could authorize it and it was inconceivable that he would; and that unauthorized revelation would make most difficult continuation of the intimate and confidential relationship between our Chiefs of Staff and theirs. The other task was to balance negation with constructive suggestion, to offer an alternative to the offending paragraphs. The last, when agreed, was written by me in red pencil diagonally across the portions to be replaced. We then broke up to get the letter typed, the speech photostated, a little rest, if possible, and to meet again for breakfast at eight o'clock. There the letter was signed and Luke sent off to Downing Street with instructions to deliver it only to the Prime Minister or his private secretary. Later on I followed the same route to the Foreign Office, across the street from No. 10, the speech in my pocket, for the last of our four-power meetings.

We had not been meeting long when the first of an expected series of messages came to me that the Prime Minister urgently wished to see me across the street. I pled inability to come until our meeting adjourned. When it did, I walked over alone. There was no doubt that I was expected, and had been for some time. I was led down the long hall flanked by busts of former tenants to the Cabinet Room at the end. It is not a large room and is overcrowded by a green baize-covered table too big for it and barely leaving room to move about behind the chairs.

Mr. Churchill was alone in the center of the near side, slumped over, his arms on the table, the picture—and, I thought, a rather carefully posed picture—of dejection.

"Good morning, sir," I said, as the usher withdrew closing the door.

"Naked before mine enemies," said Mr. Churchill, hardly looking up.

"I beg your pardon?"

"You have struck the sword from my hand," he went on as though talking to himself.

"You wished to see me, Prime Minister?" I asked. His manner changed.

"You won't let me make my speech," he said, now almost aggressively. "Here I am beset for standing by you; and you take away my only weapon."

"Not at all," I answered. "You proposed to use information which cannot be used. I have no power in the matter. Anyway, you can make a perfectly good speech without getting into secret stuff at all."

"How can I?" he asked.

"Prime Minister," I said, "I have done something so presumptuous that I hardly dare to mention it. I have edited a speech by Winston Churchill."

"Let me see it," he demanded. This would never do. To see his own work scribbled over by me might well be fatal to him.

"No," I said, "I will read it to you." And so I did. I read, as our children used to say in describing their early school exercises in reading, "with expression," blending our interpolations into his own paragraphs as much as possible. As it went on, I became rather impressed by our success or luck in catching his style. By the time we came to the end, Churchill was listening eagerly and excitedly.

"I can win with that," he broke in. "Read that first part again." This time I gave our part the full robust Churchillian treatment and rather skimped his.

"It's a bargain," he cried. "I can use that. Give it to me." I turned it over to him. He was so bubbling with pleasure that even the dreadful defacements of his script did not seem to bother him.

"Do you want another letter," he asked, "accepting your changes?"

"It's not necessary," I assured him. "Your telling me is enough."

"I like that," he said, "I like that." It was time for me to go. He walked down the hall with me to the door.

"When," he asked, "did you do all this?"

"In the only time I had," I told him, "last night between two and five. That's when I'm told you work. But," I added, "I nearly didn't look at your letter until it would have been too late."

"Yes," he said, "that was always a possibility."

January, 1953, was a month of official farewells, culminating on Inauguration Day, Tuesday, the twentieth. Among them was one to Mr. Churchill. He had crossed the ocean for a vacation in Jamaica and on the way to call on his old friend, the President-elect. On his way south he stopped to say his farewells to President Truman. Averell Harriman and I met him at the airport on January 8 and escorted him to the British Embassy. At four o'clock we met him at the White House for a call on the President. That evening at nine he entertained at a stag dinner at the Embassy for the President. None of us who attended are likely to forget it.

The President was in a gay humor, looking forward, he said, to a rest and a release from his guards, a necessary but claustrophobic restraint. Mr. Churchill seemed silent and somber, denied the relaxing effect of the cocktails, which he did not like. As we went in to dinner the gathering seemed constrained. It was a small group: besides the President and Mr. Churchill, Sir Roger Makins, who had just become Her Majesty's Ambassador, Robert Lovett, Averell Harriman, General Omar Bradley, and I, with balancing members of the Embassy staff, completed the party.

At the Prime Minister's place stood the familiar bottle of champagne. I pinned my faith to this as the needed lubricant. But before a drop of it was put to this beneficent purpose, Mr. Churchill turned to the President on his right, with devastating effect.

"Mr. President, I hope you have your answer ready for that hour when you and I stand before St. Peter and he says, 'I understand you two are responsible for putting off those atomic bombs. What have you got to say for yourselves?' "

"Oh, Lord," I thought, "here goes the evening. What a jolly subject!" Bob Lovett, a good man in a tight spot, without a second's hesitation asked very politely,

"Are you sure, Prime Minister, that you are going to be in the same place as the President for that interrogation?" This was something of a stopper. Mr. Churchill swallowed a glass of inspiration and came back vigorously.

"Lovett," he said, "my vast respect for the Creator of this universe and countless others gives me assurance that He would not condemn a man without a hearing." Bob summoned the recollection of a law school course thirty years past.

"True," he agreed with judicial detachment. "But your hearing would not be likely to start in the Supreme Court, or, necessarily, in the same court as the President's. It could

be in another court far away." By this time the President relaxed, as Mr. Churchill was obviously enjoying the performance.

"I don't know about that," he shot at Bob. "But, wherever
it is, it will be in accordance with the principles of the
English common law." It was now time for me to spell
Lovett.

"Is it altogether consistent with your respect for the Creator
of this and other universes," I asked, "to limit His imagination in judicial procedure to the accomplishment of a minute
island, in a tiny world, in one of the smaller of the universes?"

"Can you think of anything better?"

"No," I admitted, "but I don't put myself in the position
of the Creator of these universes."

"Well, there will be trial by a jury of my peers," he
announced. "That's certain." Now we were getting some-
where. Looking at Lovett, I intoned,

"Oyez! Oyez! In the Matter of the Immigration of Winston
Spencer Churchill. Mr. Bailiff, will you impanel a jury?" Bob
looked at General Bradley.

"Are you Alexander the Great?" Brad admitted that he
was. Asked whether he had formed an opinion about the
matter at issue, he inquired whether he had to tell the truth,
and was assured that, considering the place where the hearing
was held, this was not necessary. He was accepted as a peer
juror. So were Julius Caesar, Socrates, and Aristotle. Voltaire
was challenged as an atheist and Oliver Cromwell as not
believing in the fundamental law. When General G. Washington was called, Mr. Churchill paused, then—

"I waive a jury," he announced, "but not *habeas corpus*.
You'll not put me in any black hole."

The President was chosen as the judge to try the case; but
we had taken liberties enough, the evening was in no danger,
and judgment was soon given for our host.

Another issue was raised later in the evening—whether the President's merits as a statesman were overbalanced by demerits as a pianist. The latter was put to the test and won a judgment in his favor by the Prime Minister. A charge of logrolling was overruled by both of them.

That evening underlined a characteristic which these two widely different men held in common and which I greatly admired. President Roosevelt had always called the Prime Minister by his first name, as, indeed, did most of Mr. Churchill's associates in his own country. Mr. Truman never did so. Mr. Churchill invariably—and properly—addressed both Mr. Roosevelt and Mr. Truman as "Mr. President"— a mark of respect for that great office. During the evening I speak of, under the President's urging they agreed that now, as Mr. Truman's exalted status was expiring, they would use the more intimate and informal first name address. But it was no use; the habit of respect for the office or the man or both was too strong. After an embarrassed effort on each side, they relapsed into the more comfortable usage of mutual and respectful formality.

What can one say of a man of whom everything has been said, of whom every hyperbole is an understatement? One evening, on January 17, 1952, to be exact, I faced this intimidating question in introducing Prime Minister Churchill to a large official dinner in his honor in Washington. Out of panic a train of thought began to emerge. Greatness is for the mass of mankind an alienating quality. We understand by sharing an experience, but none of us have experienced greatness, or are ever likely to. We are familiar with the idea that ability, application, and virtue are said to bring their earthly reward, but find it depressing. What would give us a thrill, what would make us love a man, would be a demonstration that a first-class, magnificent error, a really crashing

folly, could pay off in a big way. This is the secret dream
of each of us, experts in error and bad luck.

To us, therefore, the salt of the earth, who would lynch
Horatio Alger if we could get our hands on him, our guest
was a natural hero. We loved him for the mistakes he had
made. An instance from his early life would illustrate. A
subaltern in an hussar regiment, he went out to India in his
teens. The troops disembarked into longboats coming alongside the quay with a sea running. On the rise of a wave,
Subaltern Churchill, in the bow of one of the boats, grasped
an iron ring set in the sea wall, a supremely stupid thing to
do, as soon appeared. The boat fell sharply as the wave re-
ceded, and Mr. Churchill writhed in the bottom of the boat
with a badly dislocated shoulder.

After some weeks it appeared that his career as a cavalry
officer had received a blight just as it began. Owing to his
crippled right shoulder, the historic cavalry officer's weapon,
the saber, was not for him. He simply could not swing it. In a
few years he was turning to a career of letters and politics.
But army life did not end before he had wangled his way to
the Sudan with the Twenty-first Lancers in Lord Kitchener's
march on Omdurman for the final crushing of Mahdism in
the Sudan.

At Omdurman, Churchill took part in one of the last
cavalry charges in the history of warfare. The casualties were
heavy. The Lancers moved forward, gathering speed, pen-
nants fluttering on their spears, their officers' sabers flashing.
Churchill could flash his saber, but could not use it in battle.
The charge crashed into the Dervish mob, lost momentum,
and nearly stopped. Lances and sabers were no better than
the weapons of the Dervishes in the resulting melee. Horses
were hamstrung; officers and soldiers butchered on the
ground. At full gallop Churchill sheathed his sword, drew

his Mauser pistol, and shot his way through the mob. If it had not been for the bad judgment and bad luck which produced that dislocated shoulder, he might have made "some corner of a foreign field . . . for ever England." As it was, he became Prime Minister of Britain in her darkest hour and saved both his country and perhaps freedom in this world.

The Prime Minister was listening eagerly and nodding. "It is true," he kept saying delightedly. Then picking up the theme, he made a gay speech extolling the bottom half of the class as the repository of leaders.

It is not within the scope of a sketch of Mr. Churchill toward the end of his official life to appraise his position in his times. That would be an intimidating task. He shared a stage on which political personalities were crowded by men in other walks of life who affected the thoughts and acts of men, and, perhaps, even more important, the effects and consequences of their acts. The rise and fall of Athens may perhaps be comprised within the wisdom and errors of Pericles and the follies and betrayals of Cleon or Alcibiades. But human conduct in the sixteenth and seventeenth centuries was affected more, I should say, by the leaders of the Reformation and Counter-Reformation than by the princes and their ministers who sought to channel these fighting faiths to their purposes. This was true also of the leaders of the Enlightenment in the eighteenth century, which produced the secular revolution of democracy. In our own day we are painfully aware that the scientific revolution has pushed mankind in directions and with velocities which have left statesmen bewildered. Often they have barely been able to avoid disaster; often they have precipitated it. But in both cases they gave, at most, a twist of guidance—more often for ill than for good—to forces they did not create. Ideas and acts which are as old as human history have taken on new force and consequence in the new state of human knowledge, as it is hardly necessary to stress in a time of nuclear power, intercontinental and interplanetary missiles, instantaneous communication, and industry based on electronics and automation. Statesmen are not less able or moral than their predecessors, though some in recent history have set new lows in the latter regard; the material with which they must work is more intractable; and too many equally able men are daily making it more intractable.

As one uncontrollable force after another has been let loose to propagate still others, man has become more and more the victim of his own creations. Yet Mr. Churchill has been one of the few—the very few—who have significantly and beneficently affected the course of events. That course would have been markedly different without him, certainly in the early 1940's. How seldom can this be truly said of anyone! We tend to obscure this truth from ourselves because, being simians, it seems to us that chatter about events must affect them, just as Chanticleer believed that his crowing made the sun rise.

Mr. Justice Holmes used to say that, as a boy, he would each year go at dawn with other boys to the circus grounds to watch the parade form in all its glamour, from the drum major and the band in front, through the elephants, the acrobats, the equestriennes, the animal cages, the clowns, to the steam calliope at the end. When the parade began, the boys, and a few stray dogs, would lead it down the main street, full of a sense of self-importance and some responsibility. As the morning wore on, however, the boys would get tired and hungry. Before long, they would turn down a side street to head for home. But the parade kept straight on.

For a time Mr. Churchill affected the line of march of the parade. By 1950 he had ceased to do this. He had aged. His lever and his fulcrum were insufficient. "Give me but one firm place on which to stand," Archimedes is supposed to have said, "and I will move the earth." In the 1950's Britain was not that place. He still had his glorious sense of words drawn from that special reservoir, from which Lincoln also drew, fed by Shakespeare and those Tudor clerics who wrote the first prayer book of Edward VI and their Jacobean successors who translated the Bible. But at the time I speak of, one began to wonder whether those sonorous words entrapped him. This seemed to me to be true about the European Army. Mr. Churchill had spoken for the idea, as an abstraction, when in opposition he was a delegate to the Council of Europe at Strasbourg in August, 1950. But, when in 1952 it seemed to be approaching reality, he was difficult. He spoke of Schuman's idea as a polyglot mob, in which soldiers without a common loyalty would not even understand one another or their officers. What he wanted, he would say, was a strong French Army singing the *"Marseillaise,"* a strong German Army singing *"Die Wacht am Rhein,"* a valiant British Army thrilling to "God Save the Queen," all bound together in the brotherly comradeship of arms. Like a bundle of faggots, each would gain strength from the rest until as a bundle they would be unbreakable.

This was sheer oratory, as he would see when it was explained to him that the formations of the EDC would not be polyglot, since through the divisional unit they would be on a national basis; that there could be no strong balanced national forces, since neither Britain nor France believed that they could afford them, nor would they permit Germany to have one; and, finally, that the people of Europe were disillusioned with the pettiness of their nationalisms and would unite only upon a broader and more hopeful loyalty. Then he would quite unjustly scold Eden for not having explained all this to him, and be seemingly in full agreement until the subject came up again later on, when he would make the same speech. But it is only fair to add that this difficulty was not translated into the field of action; his government was consistently helpful in furthering the plan for the European Defense Community.

Another instance of his being entrapped by the illusion of his own words was his phrase "conference at the summit." What began as an attractive catchphrase to mean a meeting of four heads of government gradually seduced him, and countless others, into a transcendentalism, by which such a meeting took on spiritual and superhuman potentialities. It would be held in the atmosphere of a political Parnassus, washed clean of propaganda and earthy purposefulness, where more godlike creatures could pursue, and perhaps attain, goals beyond the reach of these same beings in their daily human environment. This phrase has done singular disservice to the decade of the 1950's.

These impressions, though necessary to round out this sketch, are minor. How shall I sum up an attitude toward Mr. Churchill which I share with a large number who have worked with him, but have never been close to him? It is, I think, at bottom not very different from that combination of deep respect, veneration, and affection, warm but not intimate, which a loyal but sophisticated Catholic might have for the Pope. But it has more gaiety about it than that. For, as I hope this sketch has brought out, Mr. Churchill's immense vitality carried with it the sparkle of an inexhaustible spring.

Something of this feeling went into my note to him, when he returned the seals of office to Her Majesty and became once more a private member of Parliament. The note was dated April 7, 1955:

Dear Sir Winston,

More than ever you and Lady Churchill have been in our minds. My wife and I send you both a message of our profound respect and admiration, our affection and our warmest hopes for your happiness. There is also our gratitude and the gratitude of millions like us everywhere—gratitude for the reasons which have been said so often and for another reason. At a time when man has seemed to be dwarfed by his own creations, you have shown us anew the grandeur and greatness which the human spirit can achieve. It is by this that men live.

May all good things and only good things come to you.

Most sincerely yours,
Dean Acheson

IV

A RUSSIAN GALLERY

Until Molotov's time, said a colleague of mine, Soviet foreign ministers were minor officials, even a renegade aristocrat like George V. Ornatsky (alias Chicherin), whose function was to deal insincerely with the capitalist powers. With the war, the function did not change; but the grade of the job did. In 1939 foreign affairs ceased to be a matter of propaganda and maneuver and began to involve the survival of the regime. At that point one of the big guns, Vyacheslav Molotov, was assigned to the job. He was tough, but a poor diplomatist, outmaneuvered by Ribbentrop, and unprepared for the massive Nazi offensive mounted against the Soviet Union.

In the autumn of 1946 my chief, Secretary of State Byrnes, was in New York at the United Nations and a Conference of Foreign Ministers, battling with Molotov over a long list of disagreements from the control of atomic energy to peace treaties. Mr. Molotov had decided to celebrate the Soviet national day, the anniversary of the October Revolution—which confusingly occurs in November by our calendar—at the Soviet Embassy in Washington. He also wanted to be received by the President. In those days of man's innocence about the Russians, Mr. Byrnes did not want minor irritations to add unnecessarily to major ones. He telephoned me to take personal charge of the visit and see that no hitch or untoward incident should mar it.

So I was on hand at the Union Station with the Soviet

Ambassador to greet Molotov. These ceremonies over, he refused my invitation to drive with me in the unglamorous hand-me-down which a parsimonious government provided for the Under Secretary of State and entered the black, sleek Embassy limousine. We stood respectfully until it should drive away. As the chauffeur stepped on the starter, fire shot out of the hood, followed by a strong odor of burnt paint. Security agents swarmed around the car and cautiously looked under the hood. The trouble happily was mechanical and not political, but the car was definitely unco-operative.

Our visitor and the Ambassador joined me in my car, to the vast pleasure of the Department chauffeur, who had never had a police escort before or been able to test out the old car for speed. As we swung into Pennsylvania Avenue, he began to push the leading motorcycles. The officers put on speed and started their sirens. My car gained on them again. Again, in self-protection, they moved faster. Traffic and pedestrians scattered. At sixty miles an hour I intervened, and he did slow down as we made the S turn around the Treasury. When we pulled up at the Soviet Embassy on Sixteenth Street, he was obviously too happy to be scolded.

Molotov, in the midst of the screaming sirens, was being as affable as he could be. How was it, he shrieked in Russian, translated by Pavlov beside me, that he had not met me before at any of the wartime meetings? "Because I wasn't there." But why wasn't I there? "Mr. Hull," I said, "always gave two answers to my question why I was always left in Washington. I could, he said, take my choice. One was that he could not spare me; the other, that I needed his watchful eye upon me."

This was the sort of humor that Molotov understood. He smiled with the spontaneity of a mechanical tiger. "The Secretary," he beamed at me, "has the jolly spirit."

I did not have it long. A meeting at the White House, an

interminable reception at the Soviet Embassy, and I had
reeled home to dinner and rest, when Stanley Woodward,
Chief of Protocol, came to tell me that Mr. M. was on his way
to the station to return to New York. He did not believe
that duty required that I say farewell again on the train.
But Mr. Byrnes's admonition rang in my ears.

"Stanley," I said, "in the words of the old woman as she
put on black underwear for the funeral, 'When Ah moans,
Ah moans.'" So we went off together to say a ceremonial
farewell and to watch our visitor's train disappear down
the darkening track.

Andrei Vyshinsky was not a leading figure in the Communist hierarchy. He was no Molotov. Clever and useful, a
Menshevik, not a Bolshevik, he never did belong to the inner
circle. Cesare Borgia would have recognized his role, as Stalin
was quick to do when the purges began. Vyshinsky was the
prosecutor who produced those debasing, and, to the West,
inexplicable "confessions."

One evening, in May, 1949, during the Conference of
Foreign Ministers in Paris, he dined with our American
group at Ambassador Bruce's residence. The evening passed
pleasantly enough. Toward its end Vyshinsky started to talk
of the first time he had seen Charles Bohlen. It had been
some years before, when Bohlen was a junior officer at the
Moscow Embassy. Bohlen remembered the meeting, but said
that he had seen Mr. Vyshinsky long before that. Vyshinsky
guessed unsuccessfully a number of diplomatic receptions.
"No," said Bohlen, "it was at the Bukharin trial." Bukharin
had been a friend of Vyshinsky's, who got him condemned
to death. One of the episodes at the trial had been Vyshinsky's
production of a talisman which Bukharin's wife had sewed
in the lining of his coat to bring him luck. Vyshinsky had
taunted him on the luck which had brought him to the
prisoner's dock.

As Bohlen pronounced the name, Vyshinsky turned deathly white. "Oh," he said, "that was not a diplomatic job." Then hastily getting up, he said that it was late and he must be off. From the look of him, Bukharin's ghost went home with him.

Vyshinsky was short and slim, with quick abrupt gestures and rapid speech. He gave the impression of nervous tension. The close-cropped gray mustache, merciless blue eyes and sharply, if not finely, cut features set him apart from the stocky, peasant-faced Soviet officials and secret police agents around him.

We met first at the Palais Rose conference. Knowing his formidable courtroom reputation, I was braced for a dangerous and adroit antagonist. But neither then nor later did I find him so. Instead, he proved to be a long-winded and boring speaker, as so many Russians are. His debate held no surprises or subtleties. His great penchant, again like many Russians including Khrushchev, was for Russian fables. In retaliation, I, too, began to rely on fables and epigrams, making them up, even Russian ones, when nothing appropriate came to mind. One day, when he had made a particularly outrageous proposal, I said that to use an old American Indian saying his proposal was as full of propaganda as a dog was of fleas, only in this case it was all fleas and no dog. The laughter which followed convinced him that this would be in every paper in France by morning. He indicated that that point was mine, and went on good-naturedly to something else.

One contest we carried on enlivened those dreary meetings for me. The dining room of the Palais Rose, where our sessions took place, had three double French doors looking onto a garden. The room, though large, was crowded with staff people sitting in rows behind the Ministers and their immediate aides at the table. It became stuffy and hot. The center doors were to Vyshinsky's right and a little behind him. Being susceptible to drafts, he objected to their being opened. So I would wait until he was well launched on a speech and then motion to a most co-operative English girl, a member of the British staff, whose seat was by these doors. Very softly she would open one of them. As the reviving and balmy spring air began to restore us to consciousness, Vyshinsky would stop speaking and go into those convulsive gasps which precede a sneeze. Then out would come a fine explosive one. He would look angrily at the door, which one of his men would jump to close.

One evening he gave us a return dinner. "Us" included Ambassador Robert Murphy (then my advisor on German-Austrian affairs), Philip Jessup, Foster Dulles, and Chip Bohlen. Among the Russian guests was General Chuikov, Military Governor of the Soviet Zone of Germany and Commandant of the Soviet Sector of Berlin, a great ox of a man, his chest covered with medals—one, he pointed out, conferred by General Eisenhower. He was able, he said, to crack a man's skull with a blow of his fist. While we were having sherry, the General spoke of the French door episode with some amusement. He plainly stood in no awe of Vyshinsky. I then did an imitation of Vyshinsky speaking and being caught by the sneeze, my Russian being pure gibberish, made up as I went along. The General bellowed, slapped his thigh, and spoke to the interpreter. "The General," said he, "says 'begin at the beginning and do it all over again.'" He kept me at it until dinner was announced. Vyshinsky's smile became forced.

Six months later I crossed the General's trail again, this time in Berlin. The brief thaw of May had passed and by November a political freeze was on again. General Maxwell Taylor, then Commandant of our Sector in Berlin, had a reception for me to which the other three Commandants were, of course, invited. General Chuikov, he said, would not come; he had not attended any Western social function for months. I offered a ten-dollar bet that he would. General Taylor took it. The reception had been going for an hour and my chances seemed pretty dim. Then there was a great clatter at the door and in came, not only General Chuikov, but all his staff. (General Taylor refused to pay a bonus for staff.)

While we were exchanging noisy greetings and he was demanding the Vyshinsky speech, up came a waiter with a tray of cocktails, a large tray. Chuikov took a solemn appraising look and began to drink them, before I realized his mistaken assumption of a challenge.

"You don't have to drink all those, General," I assured him. "They're for everybody." He looked immensely relieved. "Good Lord," I went on. "You must have a tin stomach." It was translated. He shook his head.

"No," he said, "steel." Of course, none of this jollity meant anything or had the slightest effect on events.

Probably because he was excluded from the Soviet command, Vyshinsky took special pride in cultural attainments which his more vigorous and boorish superiors did not share. Among them was music. One evening during a session of the United Nations General Assembly in New York my wife found herself seated beside him at a pleasant dinner given by the Danish Foreign Minister at the Hotel Pierre. The Haas Orchestra was playing during dinner, choosing pieces from the great composers of the countries represented at the dinner. Vyshinsky began to talk of the trios played by his wife, their daughter, and himself, of his extensive knowledge of Russian music, and of the superiority of Russian composers. My wife spoke of her great admiration of Russian music, but regretted that her knowledge of the younger men, Shostakovich and Prokofiev, for instance, was limited. She asked him to draw her attention to any Russian music which might be played.

Later on, while talking with her other neighbor, she heard the orchestra begin a piece from Tschaikovsky's *Romeo and Juliet*. She turned to Vyshinsky and asked him, innocently, if he could identify the piece for her. He listened carefully and could not. She then could and did, to his considerable confusion. A year later at Trygve Lie's house on Long Island after luncheon the same orchestra began the waltz from *Swan Lake*. Vyshinsky was across the room. Instantly he left his partner, walked across the room to my wife, bowed formally, and said in French, "They play the Tschaikovsky well, do they not?"

Why is it that so many of us who have dealt with Russian officials find that personal recollections are pretty much restricted to anecdotes, sardonic or ridiculous, to discussions, frustrating and boring? It is, I think, because no real personal relations are possible. Either those Russians with whom we have had to deal do not dare open their minds, or those who dare have nothing in them to disclose.

Sir William Hayter, formerly British Ambassador in Moscow, has come to the same conclusion. With individual Russians, he has written in the London *Observer* (October 2, 1960), it is not "possible to establish any kind of lasting or genuine personal relationship," and with "the real rulers of Russia . . . it was the distressing experience of all Ambassadors that these great men had no more to say in private than in public; the same series of gramophone records was played on every occasion; nothing emerged from these private conversations that could not just as well be gleaned from the pages of *Pravda*."

It seems almost as though Russians going abroad went to a school of dialectics, where naturally coarse manners were made intentionally offensive, and where the students were trained in a technique of intellectual deviousness designed to frustrate any discussion. For instance, if one is inexperienced enough to be involved in discussion of the merits of free thought, free expression, and a free press, the riposte is that our information media are owned and used by the imperialist-monopolists to poison and misinform the masses. How much better the wise parent who forces his children to speak the truth by punishing them when they tell falsehoods. Even better, we are told, is the Soviet government which makes the truth so abundantly available to all citizens that there is no need or place for private versions and perversions of it. This same pattern of thought can be applied to elections, in which the same benevolent Soviet system safeguards the ingenuous elector from the misguidance of self-interested and ambitious men, by permitting only one candidate—in other words "the best man." After a few evenings of this sort of talk, anything is preferable.

In official negotiations the methods employed have a common root. My discovery of it, and consequent saving of my sanity, I owe to Averell Harriman. Toward the end of the war I found myself the head of an American group negotiating with a Russian group for the delivery and payment of some war surplus property when hostilities should stop. After the third meeting it dawned on me that the Russians were merely repeating the same things and that we were getting nowhere. I disclosed my frustration to Averell, our Ambassador then to Moscow, who was in Washington for consultation.

"Take a few days' recess," he advised, "then meet, give them a paper with your proposal, explain it, and recess again. This will enable them to cable Moscow and get instructions." He explained that none of our oral proposals had been sent to Moscow, since to have done so would have opened the sender to charges of being impressed by what we said, but that a written proposal was another thing. This had to be reported. To suppress it would be to assume responsibility which also could lead to criticism. This advice worked. The negotiations got nowhere; but they ended, of which there had seemed to be no possibility before.

The personal and social hours, which were of such vast importance in working out arrangements with our Allies, were of no use with the Russians, and were a weariness of the flesh. Any device to pass the time was eagerly grasped. Such a device came to me on what promised to be a grisly evening at Trygve Lie's home on Long Island, during the General Assembly session of the autumn of 1950.

In a way the whole affair was my fault, though Governor Thomas E. Dewey of New York had a generous hand in it. We have been friends for many years. I am deeply indebted to the Governor for strong support when I most needed it. He would, I think, agree that we have always dealt with one another frankly and with sympathetic understanding. So, when he called me on the telephone one afternoon in New York and read me a short speech he proposed to make at the Mayor's dinner that night for the chiefs of mission to the General Assembly, I gave him my best, but hasty, judgment in saying that it sounded all right. But I was wrong.

Unfortunately, it contained language critical of the Soviet Union, which, though mild compared to what Vyshinsky was saying daily about us, should not have been said by an official host about an official guest. Vyshinsky and his Russians walked out of the Waldorf and complained officially, with the result that I had to express official regret. To have said that I had heard and approved Tom Dewey's speech would only have made matters worse. But I explained the facts to the President, said that the Governor was free to state them, if he wished, and added that, if any of our own people attacked him, I would come to his defense. This cooled off the political enthusiasts; and the Governor took the gentle press reproofs in his stride.

In this posture of events Trygve Lie, Secretary General of the United Nations, gave a dinner for the attending Foreign Ministers, insisting that I should attend and be especially agreeable to Vyshinsky. That evening I set out resignedly from my Waldorf Tower prison in the official limousine, competently guarded by two security officers. Very soon the evening began to take on a fairytale unreality.

We were purring along some broad and indistinguishable Brooklyn avenue, when the most hair-raising sounds issued from under the car's hood, as though at the same moment every bearing in the engine had run dry of oil and shrieked in agonized protest. The chauffeur, who had driven Secretary Charles Evans Hughes and all his successors—and still (1961) does—swerved his beloved chariot to the curb and stopped the engine. This did not, oddly enough, stop the shrieks. We all got out to watch the unveiling of the mystery. Passing citizens joined us. The hood was raised; and there, on top of the engine, was one of the Waldorf garage kittens, who had sought a quiet rest and gotten the hot-foot treatment. My guards, who were prepared, in the words of St. Paul, to "quench all the fiery darts of the wicked" in my defense, were utterly baffled by a small kitten. To abandon a Waldorf kitten in Brooklyn would never do. No offers of adoption came from the delighted crowd. So we agreed that one of the guards should put it in his pocket and, after it had dined in Lie's kitchen, return it to its mother's quarters in the garage.

At dinner I found myself on one side of the hostess—on this occasion Lie's charming daughter—with Vyshinsky on her other side. The episode of the kitten kept all of us out of trouble for a time. Then we listened to an account of how hard Vyshinsky worked and at Churchillian hours between midnight and dawn. Several of us complained mildly of our lot. We should, I suggested idly, form a trade union, since in all countries we seemed to be an exploited group, underpaid, overworked, and universally abused. Interest began to grow and our conversation broadened up the table; Miss Lie was having a good time.

Vyshinsky demurred to a trade union. In the Soviet Union they were not necessary to protect the workers, he said, since that was the principal purpose of the state. Soviet trade unions stimulated production. That settled it, Miss Lie decided. We could not have a Soviet-style trade union because Mr. Vyshinsky was by his own statement already over-stimulated and overworked, as were all foreign ministers and secretaries general. So we must have an old-fashioned, reactionary trade union to protect the members. Mr. Vyshinsky, she thought, would be just the man to head it up. This was impossible, he said, because he would have to be nominated —and who would do that?—and elected, when we all knew that the vote in the Assembly was always 45 to 5 against Soviet proposals, as indeed at that time it was.

Our gallant hostess deserved help. As for the nomination, I said, I would do that myself, and do it there and then. The election would depend on our joint efforts, for not only must I present the candidate in a favorable light, but he must do the same thing in his acceptance. No doctrinal dissertation would do; he must go all out for votes. All interest at the table had by this time centered on our end of it. The Secretary General, who had no idea what was going on, looked worried but not agitated, as his daughter was obviously enjoying herself. In answer to his puzzled look, Miss Lie announced that Mr. Acheson was about to nominate Mr. Vyshinsky to lead the newly formed trade union of foreign ministers. Mr. Vyshinsky's speech of acceptance would follow.

I rose and addressed the convention, while our hostess held up the next course. Only the opening sentence now comes back to me across the years. "Foreign Ministers of the World, unite! You have nothing to lose but your chains of office!" The theme, of course, was our pitiable condition, the brutality of our exploitation and oppressors, who were the entire population of the self-governing world, and the qualifications of our peerless leader, a veritable David, who with a smooth pebble from the brook would smite this Goliath.

Vyshinsky very good-naturedly did his part. I wish I could say that it was with gay burlesque of our great American political institution, the nominating convention. But caution intervened. Whether because M.V.D. men lurked among his guards, or fear of leaks to the press came to his mind, he played it in a low key. But Trygve Lie's purpose had been achieved. For one evening tensions were relaxed.

Years before this, another attempt at hands-across-the-iron-curtain almost ended in a brawl precipitated by the odd behavior of a British diplomat. It was at the conference in Atlantic City in November, 1943, on postwar relief and re-habilitation. The Russian delegation was headed by a young Vice Commissar for Trade, Vasili A. Sergeev, a child of the new regime and, as I recall it, of a steelworker. Sergeev was both bright and agreeable. An altogether delightful character led the British group, John J. Llewellin (later Lord Llewellin, Governor General of the Federation of Rhodesia and Nyasa-land), then Minister of Food. Llewellin was the perfect John Bull, solid, florid, given to unbelievable banalities and to ejaculations without meaning, like "My word!" and "Oh, I say!" But he had good common sense, inexhaustible good nature, and nothing really surprised him.

After the conference had shaken down a bit—the shaking fell to me as its Chairman—Sergeev announced to us that the Russians wished to entertain the British and American groups at a dinner for which they had brought by air caviar and vodka. As Atlantic City was my second experience of Russians at conferences, I was aware that they came equipped with these staples, but to Llewellin it was the delightfully right luggage for the leading applicant for postwar relief. We, of course, accepted for our colleagues, who had nothing better to do anyway.

Russian dinners, at that time, had two tiresome accompaniments which were not made more agreeable by being combined. These were an adolescent eagerness for drinking competitions, as such; and the proposing *ad infinitum* of toasts. The only escape, often to the relief of the hosts, was to plead stomach ulcers, or more obscure gastric complaints, which restricted one to mild and diluted beverages. On this evening, however, Sergeev had the bit in his teeth and would tolerate no evasions. From the interminable *hors d'oeuvres* of caviar on thick toast with vodka, all the way through dinner, we toasted until the imagination boggled at new candidates. As, toward dessert, a diplomat, who shall be nameless, rose, the noisy room quieted to hear a Slavic expert. Holding the black ribbon of his *pince-nez,* he spoke with immense pomposity.

"The toasts we have had this evening," he began, "have been to men and organizations of men—to our leaders at home and in the field, and to those they lead to a glorious victory. I will give you an event, a potent event, an event which has done more to bring the Soviet people close to our countrymen, the British and American peoples, than anything we can think of. I give you June 22, 1941, the day Hitler attacked the Soviet Union!" John Russell of the British Foreign Service was translating as the speech went along. Without batting an eye he rendered that last sentence, "I give you the glorious resistance of the Soviet people since the day of Hitler's ignominious attack."

At once a half-dozen Russians who were supposed to speak no English roared in angry dissent. "He did not say that." When they explained to their comrades what had been said, they joined the growing pandemonium. It began to look as though the iron curtain would come down with a bang.

At this point Jay Llewellin rose none too steadily and gaveled the meeting to an approximation of order with a large spoon. "Some say one thing," he announced judiciously, "and some say another. I wasn't listening and don't know. What's more, I don't give a damn. Let's stop all this and have a jolly Russian song." With that, he changed the function of the spoon from gavel to baton and started bellowing the Volga Boatmen's song. As we all, even the Russians, joined in, John Russell jumped on the table and did a Cossack dance, including the leg kicks from a squat. The Russians clapped the tune and beat on the table. John's kicks sent dishes, glasses, and silver flying. In a minute the Russian mood had changed. This was fun. This was the way a party should be. And it is the way it was—until the management mercifully broke it up. The next day we voted Johnny Russell the Lenin Medal for Life Saving, First Class.

My first experience of Russians at conferences was at the Conference on Food and Agriculture at Virginia Hot Springs in 1943. President Roosevelt had the bizarre idea of using the barbed wire and Marine guards, designed to keep the Axis diplomats in, for the converse end of keeping the press out. Why this was done was never clear to those involved, including Congressman Marvin Jones of Texas, Chairman of the conference, later Chief Judge of the Court of Claims. Never was any meeting more innocent of secret information or of strategic purposes. At times, it seemed innocent of any purposes. Nevertheless, exclusion produced irritation, and, along with it, a lot of imaginative stories which caused mounting congressional concern.

Secretary of State Hull sent me down there to find out what the trouble was. The answer was fairly obvious—to open gaps in the barbed wire—but the trip offered a pleasant change from Washington. Among the firsts which this experience brought me was the Russian *nyet* in person. I can still hear the Russian interpreter translating his chief. "Mr. Krutikov, he says no." Another first was the caviar and vodka party with its adolescent background.

A good friend made during that visit, Mr. Richard Law of the British delegation, now Lord Coleraine, a son of Bonar Law, told me of its aftermath. In the room directly under Law in the Homestead, and identical with his, was a gigantic Soviet agricultural expert. He had the longest arms I have ever seen and a shambling gait which gave him unmistakable resemblance to a gorilla. Law left the party as soon as he decently could, went to bed and to sleep. Hours later he was awakened by the sound of something moving in his room. He tried sleepily to pierce the darkness. Dimly he saw a mountainous apelike creature.

"The vodka," he thought. "I'll blink my eyes and it will go away." When he looked again, it was almost above him. "Help!" he shouted. "Get out of here!" There was a great scrambling. The door flew open and down the corridor fled the agricultural expert carrying his clothes and shoes.

As the "hate America" campaign grew in fury during 1951 and 1952, its vilification of our leaders and our people, the germ warfare accusations, and the barbarities of the Chinese prisoner-of-war camps ended even such amenities as I have described, if they can be called that. My encounters with Vyshinsky in those years were restricted to debate during sessions of the General Assembly of the United Nations, both in plenary meetings and in committee meetings. The accident of English alphabetical seating put the U.S.A. between U.K. and U.S.S.R., so that in the smaller meetings we actually sat side by side. In the larger ones, aides would separate us. The custom in the Political Committee, where most of the work of the session was done, of speaking seated in one's place, rather than from a podium, as in the General Assembly, had the curious result of having my opponent almost in my lap, all my notes spread out before him (in Vyshinsky's case, no embarrassment), and a sweeping gesture likely to sweep him off his chair. The practice of allowing photographers to wander at will before the meetings convened made it desirable to arrive late and escape the embarrassment of being told to shake hands and grin.

In these debates my impression of 1949, that Vyshinsky was not effective, was borne out again. It was strange that this was so because the man had ability. But, judged both from the point of view of his effect on the delegates and his world propaganda effect, he was a failure. At the 1951 session in Paris I put forward our government's broad and comprehensive plan for the control and limitation of armaments, the first effort of this kind since the proposals for the international control of atomic energy in 1946. This proposal for staged advances in both reduction and control of all armaments was of the utmost importance, as all the delegates recognized at once. Indeed, it is still pretty much the core of all Western proposals made since. Everyone was aware that any such plan bristled with difficulties requiring years of negotiation. But this serious start on what many regarded as the number one problem of our time dominated the thinking of the delegates.

Vyshinsky spoke the next day. Overnight Foreign Ministers had thrown away their prepared speeches to address themselves to this new center of all interest. Vyshinsky spoke to a hall crowded to hear the Soviet Union's response to the American lead. He had, so he said, laughed all night! The utter and cynical frivolity of this response stunned the

Assembly. As he went on to heap ridicule upon the plan and upon the motives of those who proposed it, a sense of deep anger grew throughout the audience. In a few days the same anger was apparent in the greater world audience. Vyshinsky had bungled his case.

A year later he did it again—this time in a much hotter debate. The issue was whether the General Assembly would approve an armistice in Korea which included, as the Russians and Chinese Communists demanded, a provision for the forced return of prisoners of war to their own side, or, as we insisted, the right of the prisoner to choose whether to go back or go where else he could.

In the early stages we handled this issue and the whole prisoner-of-war matter badly. It was not mentioned at all in the first informal and highly secret talks in which an armistice was broached. We did not know that a problem of return existed. The Russians may have been aware of its existence and construed our failure to raise it as an intentional waiver. At any rate, when we did learn of the problem and raised the issue, we were met by exceptional virulence from the North Koreans and Chinese. This was only the beginning of our troubles. Quite obviously our Army had not placed its ablest officers in charge of the prisoner-of-war camps, with the result that the Communist prisoners instigated riots and attacks on defectors, in one case taking over the camp and capturing the commanding officer. By the time order was restored and the prisoners were classified and separated, Communist propaganda was charging us with manufacturing the whole issue and coercing prisoners into defecting.

Our experience after World War II in forcing defecting prisoners to return, many of whom chose suicide to torture and execution, determined us to have no more of this degrading traffic in human beings. When we once knew the facts and the issue, we were adamant. In this atmosphere the debate took place in the Political Committee, to which the matter of armistice terms had been referred. This committee was really a committee of the whole, comprising the whole membership of the United Nations.

Never was I more impressed with the importance of thorough preparation and unrestricted time in making clear even a complex situation, intentionally confused. I had Vyshinsky and Krishna Menon of India against me, but I had the opening speech. It would have been suicide to read a manuscript to that audience. For nearly three hours, guided by notes and using, where helpful, actual documents, I traced the attack on South Korea, the position taken by the United Nations, the facts about the prisoner-of-war issue, and the relevant rules of law and practice of nations, which were not wholly uniform.

Vyshinsky had overlooked, or thought we had, a group of Soviet treaties at the end of World War I which did just what he now said was unlawful and unprecedented. At that time, there were considerable numbers of Eastern European prisoners of war in Russia who had thrown in their lot with the Communist revolution and wanted to stay in the Soviet Union, since to go home was to court reprisals and very probably death. Each of these treaties I brought out separately, reading all the relevant passages in full and comparing them to Mr. Vyshinsky's present position. This appeared to disconcert him considerably.

The effort was one in exposition, not oratory. At the end of it Sir Muhammad Zafrulla Khan, Foreign Minister of Pakistan, now a Judge of the International Court of Justice, said to me, "I had no idea the case was so strong." Telling the whole story brought its own compulsion.

Vyshinsky replied for four hours, and Menon for about one. Most of Vyshinsky's argument was a repetition of familiar charges of South Korean and United States aggression, followed by a pretty good argument of the precedent against our view. Menon reinforced the latter. (His purpose was to compromise the issue obscurely.) I then took two hours or so to rebut and to close.

My argument was devoted to stating the essence of Vyshinsky's position. It was a wholly consistent position for a Communist, but an odd one for Mr. Menon. It was, of course, that a Communist state owned its people, in or out of uniform. Their demand for the return of all the prisoners of war regardless of the interests of the men as individuals was the announcement of a sort of fugitive slave act. Was this a posture which the United Nations could seriously consider? It could not, and did not.

No, Mr. Vyshinsky was not a formidable opponent. He was not equipped, as is Khrushchev, to use debate, discussion, and negotiation for their chief function in Soviet strategy. Unfortunately what this function is, is ill understood in non-Communist countries. I have heard people who should know better, including a head of government, say happily, "As long as we keep them talking, they're not fighting." Nothing could be more untrue: they are fighting. They are adopting a tactic specifically prescribed by Lenin to delay the crises while demoralizing and weakening the enemy. To our minds international conferences and international negotiations are so completely means for ending conflict that we are blind to the fact that they may be and, in the hands of experts, are equally adapted to continuing it. In the present century the Soviet state has perfected the use of negotiation, including negotiation by mass conference, as a method of warfare; this use long antedates the Communists. A classic example is the negotiation conducted at Canton by the Chinese with Lord Napier of Merchiston, representing the British government, in the 1830's, as brilliantly told by Maurice Collis in *Foreign Mud.**

* Alfred A. Knopf (New York, 1947).

The similar use of negotiation by the Communists at Brest-Litovsk in 1917–1918 and Panmunjom in 1951–1953 was worthy of the model.

Negotiation, in the classic diplomatic sense, assumes parties more anxious to agree than to disagree; parties who are, therefore, willing to make concessions in determining what shall be agreed upon. But, as a friend put it, Americans in recent years have come to see three elements in the process of negotiation. There is the element of the high school debate, in which the judges are the newspaper columnists and the Asian and African leaders are the audience. In other words, this element stresses the impression made by the negotiation, often a contrived impression, as in the Geneva Summit Meeting of 1955, rather than its outcome. The second element is the Yankee horsetrade. Here the emphasis is on outmaneuvering the opponent, on the game, rather than on any importance of the game.

The third element is the evangelical one of a revival meeting. Take the sawdust trail to salvation or suffer damnation in the fires of a nuclear hell. "There is no alternative to negotiations with the Russians" is the constant theme of a well-known columnist and a prominent politician in this country and of a large section of the British Labour party. This is, of course, silly. For if there is no alternative, and if the Russians will only negotiate, as is now the case, on their own terms, then there is no alternative to surrender. But there plainly is an alternative, which is by action to change the attitude of the other party. Negotiation should not be, as some conceive it, mere talk apart from action. Negotiation and action are parts of one whole. Action is often the best form of negotiation. It affects the environment, which in large part is likely to determine the outcome of negotiation. The sputniks were powerful moves in negotiation; so was the Marshall Plan. Mr. Khrushchev at the 1960 Paris Summit

Meeting, as at the New York General Assembly, was affecting the environment of international relations. He was using conference and the forms of negotiation as an instrument of war.

True negotiation with the Russians, when and how it can occur, has been admirably summed up by Sir William Hayter in the excellent article already mentioned:

> Negotiation with the Russians does occur, from time to time, but it requires no particular skill. The Russians are not to be persuaded by eloquence or convinced by reasoned arguments. They rely on what Stalin used to call the proper basis of international policy, the calculation of forces. So no case, however skilfully deployed, however clearly demonstrated as irrefutable, will move them from doing what they have previously decided to do; the only way of changing their purpose is to demonstrate that they have no advantageous alternative, that what they want to do is not possible. Negotiations with the Russians are therefore very mechanical; and they are probably better conducted on paper than by word of mouth.

V

LISBON: BACKGROUND OF A
CONFERENCE

February 19–26, 1952

In mid-February, 1952, we flew into Lisbon for a NATO
Council meeting. Lovely days they were. Mists, rising from
the Tagus River and drawing a chilly shroud around the city,
were burned away at mid-morning by a bright, warm sun.

My wife and I were staying with the American Ambassador,
Lincoln MacVeagh, at the Embassy residence on one of the
seven hills of Lisbon in an old part of the city. It is an old
part because it is on a hill. Most of the city had lain in a
valley running down to the Tagus. All of this and twenty
thousand people perished in the great earthquake, fire, and
tidal wave of 1755. The Ambassador was a friend from school
days. He was one of those citizen ambassadors, now all too
few, who recapture the early days of the Republic when all
our diplomatic agents were amateurs—Franklin, the Adamses,
Jefferson, John Jay, and so on—because there were no pro-
fessionals and because they had no equals. A quiet gentleman,
a wise and cultivated man, and an undiluted Scot in observation and negotiation, Lincoln MacVeagh was always just
where he should be when he was needed: in Iceland, when
an Icelandic base became a prime necessity to meet Hitler's
submarine warfare; moved to Greece, he went through the
latter years of the war and the years of exile to be ready to
guide us through the intricacies and pitfalls of our hastily

improvised program to rescue Greece from Communist subversion and attack; he came to Portugal just in time for the
negotiation of NATO and the Azores Defense Agreement;
and finally to Spain to work out our base agreement there. If
proof were needed, as it is not, that transfusion of non-career
blood is good for the Foreign Service, Lincoln MacVeagh
would furnish it. Unfortunately his blood type is all too rare.

He undertook at once our education about Portugal and
Lisbon. We quickly caught his affection for both, first of all
from the residence itself, with its ample, frumpy, friendly
serenity. Flush with the sidewalk on a narrow street, it surrounded a well from ground to roof, around which circled
tiers of galleries. The effect of the well-like court was to give a
sense of spaciousness and to make the house next to impossible
to heat. The attempt was made, partly by a system of primitive
design and negligible efficiency, but principally by Portuguese
fireplace stoves with iron hoods which drawn down produced
a fearful draft and blaze. The old house carried an assurance,
typically Portuguese, that nothing was urgent.

With our arrival began the familiar struggle with the
security police to get a morning walk. They always disapproved of this, avowedly because it was an invitation to
disaster, but really—I always suspected—because they disliked
walking. Sometimes these struggles produced unexpected and
undesirable results. In Rome the battle had centered around
my desire to walk through the beautiful Borghese Park.
Stubbornness won the day. The next morning I pointed out
to my guards how unwarranted their fears had been, since
the park seemed deserted at that hour except for a few people
over by one of the entrances. Noticing an exchange of smiles,
I cross-examined to discover that everyone had been driven
out of the park. This had to be stopped at once, and happily
was.

The Portuguese police were more compliant. Our first

morning was a great success, down the hill, through a series of narrow and interesting little streets, all washed clean every night, and around the circle where the Marques de Pombal in bronze, high on his granite pedestal, surveys one of Europe's most glorious avenues, the Avenida da Liberdade. After the earthquake, Pombal, the Prime Minister of Joseph I, put thousands of people and oxcarts to work leveling the rubble to restore the lower town. The Avenida has a broad central roadway, bordered on each side by a strip of tree-lined parking in the center of which water flows, disappearing under cross streets and reappearing again bearing flotillas of swans. Again on each side of these strips are streets to serve the great houses and apartments which line the Avenida. In any contest for the most beautiful man-made mile, I would enter the Avenida da Liberdade.

At its downhill end it jogs past the National Theater to Black Horse Square, where Joseph I on horseback, flanked on three sides by exquisite eighteenth-century colonnaded buildings, looks over the broad Tagus to distant blue mountains.

On the second morning, however, things were different. Word gets around in Lisbon. We had made our way down the hill and entered a street with the delightful name of Largo do Rato, or Square of the Mouse, where, in an instant, advance and retreat were cut off by hundreds of children, who demanded the ransom of autographs. While I signed my arm into numbness, reinforcements were sent for, which eventually made a way for us through this juvenile sea. After that, security really cracked down. We had to leave the residence each morning by car, preceded and followed by police cars, for a destination determined by the Ambassador at the moment, from which we walked to an equally unpredictable rendezvous. I was told that betting pools were made on the general area of these walks.

My wife, unencumbered by these restrictions, soon became a well-known and popular Lisbon figure. People like watching painters at work almost as much as they do people digging a hole in the earth. Since this painter's work was done between social engagements, essential equipment was a small car and a Portuguese chauffeur. Starting early for some function, they would pick a paintable spot and park the car at a vantage point, usually illegally. The chauffeur got out to patrol and to talk with all passers-by. The painter stayed in the car with canvas propped from knees to dashboard, paint box on the seat beside her, and worked fast.

The chauffeur's pride in his charge led to some inflation of her reputation in the worlds of art, society, and diplomacy as he enlarged upon it. A crowd soon gathered and freely discussed both the painting taking form before them and the artist. Inevitably the moment arrived when someone asked whether she spoke Portuguese.

"Does she speak Portuguese?" the chauffeur would answer. "Listen to this." He would walk over to the window and ask a question in Portuguese. The lady would answer in the basic Spanish she had learned in the Cabinet wives' Spanish class. The crowd would roar in delighted amusement, urging the chauffeur to continue. But the lady enforced a strict quota. Gaiety could disrupt work.

The climax of the drama came, quite properly, at its end, when the time came to go on. Paints were packed up and stored with the canvas in the boot. A bit of tissue paper was dipped in turpentine. Working in the confines of the front seat, with brushes often held between her teeth, even a careful and tidy painter could get little daubs of paint on nose, cheeks, ears, often undetectable in the mirror of her compact. The chauffeur had the last word in "operation clean-up," with eager and vocal assistance from the sidewalk superintendents; then with make-up applied, veil down, and white gloves on, she waved good-by amid hearty cheers.

Soon after our arrival in Lisbon a state dinner for all the delegates was given by Dr. Salazar in that gem of architecture the Palace of Queluz, which means "What light." The air is supposed to be particularly clear and the light dazzling at the spot outside Lisbon where the palace, a pink Portuguese Versailles, was built. On the night of the dinner it was breathtakingly beautiful, silver-pink under the moon, with all its flood-lit fountains playing.

We came into the palace grounds by the main entrance leading to its central court, seldom used in favor of a postern gate better adapted to the control of tourists. This evening the drive was lighted by flares a few feet apart held by soldiers in eighteenth-century uniforms. The palace itself was ablaze with light, its white and gold boisserie and incomparable crystal chandeliers gleaming. The flowers in every room were arrestingly beautiful. We learned that they had had Dr. Salazar's personal attention and that, since as a boy he had helped his father in his work as a gardener, he had a great knowledge and love of flowers.

General Omar Bradley, Chairman of the Joint Chiefs of Staff, a member of the United States group, was always being furnished by the U.S. Army with recondite information. This he generously shared with the rest of us, but differed from us by usually acting on it. We, whose connection with the Army had, for the most part, been at a low level, believed army intelligence was usually wrong and not to be taken seriously. So this particular evening we disregarded the warning that the palace was unheated, would be damp and cold, and wise men—women not being subject to such weakness—should come with a wool base. But not the General. Under his heavy dress uniform, encrusted with gold braid and medals, he wore long woolen underwear and a sweater. But Dr. Salazar in his concern for our comfort was several laps ahead of army intelligence. Every gas and electric heater in Lisbon had been rounded up and put to work; every fireplace was blazing; every room was in the high seventies and getting hotter. By the time we had passed through the receiving line, General Bradley looked like a snowman in a February thaw. He was led off by encircling officers to shed clothes in an eighteenth-century palace built before our conceptions of privacy existed.

The dinner was, to my mind, a most enjoyable one because of a radical difference from another dinner I remember in an even more beautiful setting. It was Prime Minister de Gasperi's dinner three months before for the same group in the Villa Madama on the outskirts of Rome. This Renaissance villa of the greatest delicacy had been designed by Raphael and decorated by him and his pupil, Giulio Romano, in 1520 on the commission of a Medici Pope for a lady. I found myself seated beside a member of the Italian Cabinet. The conversation started bumpily. So I suggested that he consider three questions which had been puzzling me, and talk about them when he was ready. They were: Would you like to have been the Cardinal responsible for raising the money or procuring the labor to build this building? Do you wish that it had not been built? Do you think Raphael would enjoy this dinner party?

For a course of the dinner he gave thought to these problems; then answered them all in the negative. The first and second he thought fairly easy. This beauty had been created out of the sweat and labor, perhaps forced labor, of peasants. He would not want to have the doing of that job entered against him on St. Peter's books. But ancient wrongs and suffering lose their poignancy by the erosion of time. We no longer weep for Hecuba and the Trojan women. So that, even if he could expunge past sins and sorrows by the loss of present loveliness, he would not do it. The last question was not hard to answer; but it had taken longer to think why he was so sure that Raphael would not have been thrilled to join us; perhaps, because it was so obvious. There were no ladies. Almost equally distressing to Raphael there were no artists. We were all of a kind—hard, purposeful people, bent on talking about things, getting things done, which Raphael would find far more dull than even the politics of Italian city-states. In Raphael's day princes knew beauty and gave its practitioners in all the arts honor and opportunity. I gave the Minister top rating on his answers. But that evening at Queluz there were ladies present, ladies of beauty and wit, in the forefront of whom was my delightful partner, a former Portuguese Ambassadress at the Court of St. James's.

One morning the Ambassador got word that Dr. Salazar would be happy to receive us at an hour named. I was eager to meet this remarkable man, the nearest approach in our time to Plato's philosopher-king. During the war our government had extended negotiations and dealings with Dr. Salazar, then Prime Minister, Foreign Minister, and Minister of War, in an effort to deny Germany and obtain for the Allies as much of Portugal's production as possible, and later on to obtain base rights in the Azores. I had had some part in these negotiations and acquired deep respect for Dr. Salazar's competence.

His story was itself enough to quicken interest. The only son of a peasant family in Northern Portugal, his education had been the special concern of his capable mother. He studied first for the priesthood at a Jesuit seminary but soon changed to economics and law at Coimbra University. Quickly taking his bachelor's and doctor's degrees, he became a full professor with publications to his credit by 1916. Meanwhile Portugal, in turmoil and bankruptcy, rapidly approached anarchy. Salazar's venture in politics and election to the Cortes in 1921 ended after one session in his return, disgusted, to Coimbra. A succession of weak governments, interspersed with the assassination of a monarch and a crown prince and the abolition of the monarchy itself in 1911, produced the army coup of 1926 and the joint dictatorship of Generals Gomes da Costa and Carmona.

But the Army soon learned that it was simpler to seize power than to exercise it. The treasury was empty and the printing presses had lost their magic. So the Generals brought Professor Salazar to Lisbon as Minister of Finance. After two days' investigation, the Professor asked for full financial powers, including power over the military budget. The Generals refused. The Professor returned to his classroom. Two years later General Carmona had disposed of his colleague and become President. Again the Professor was brought to Lisbon, this time with the assurance of the powers he believed essential. Four years later the *escudo* was one of the world's strongest currencies, all of Portugal's foreign debt had been paid, and the country was enjoying prosperity unknown for decades.

Dr. Salazar exercises supreme power, but it is not his power in the sense that the power Stalin exercised was his. In Portugal the armed forces are in control. Dr. Salazar is their agent for government with full powers. These powers are exercised on behalf of an economic system satisfactory to the middle class from which come the officers. Both the armed forces and the Prime Minister recognize and respect the relationship and are indispensable to one another. It is indisputable that political liberty, as it is known, say, in Great Britain and the United States, does not exist in Portugal. It is equally indisputable that the Portuguese destroyed their own liberties by their misuse of them. Several times the Salazar regime has moved toward permitting political opposition but has drawn back when it approached the sort of test which Mr. Churchill risked and lost in 1945, and Lincoln risked, and expected to lose, in 1864. A libertarian may properly disapprove of Dr. Salazar, but I doubt whether Plato would —though he might worry as to what may happen when the Doctor's great abilities are no longer available.

Dr. Salazar's office in a government building was one flight up, on what we would call the second floor and Europeans, the first floor. We entered on the side by Dr. Salazar's own entrance, guarded only by an old uniformed doorman, and were taken up in a paneled, far-from-modern elevator by a young aide. "We" consisted of the Ambassador and myself and Ted Xanthaky of the embassy staff, a truly gifted as well as instantaneous interpreter. Hardly more than a word or two behind, he put into his translation the emotion of the speaker, as well as his words, so that humor, irony, solemnity, all seemed to come directly from the principals without an intermediary. As soon as our hats and coats were taken, we were shown into Dr. Salazar's connecting study. The room, of medium size, was lined on three sides with books and paintings above them, and furnished with a desk and upholstered leather chairs. I saw no telephone, files, or papers on the desk, none of the humorous figures and framed mottoes in which Presidents Roosevelt and Truman delighted. Everything about both rooms was nonofficial, comfortable, simple, and unpretentious.

At the door a slight and very handsome man smiled a welcome to us. A long and thoughtful face, topped by short-cut, graying hair, was given both a melancholy and quizzical cast by mobile eyebrows arched toward their inner ends. His manner, easy yet dignified and serious, did not suggest authority or the faintest trace of pomposity. As we sat down, exchanging the opening amenities of conversation, he sank into his chair until his crossed knee was almost level with his shoulders. With elbows rested on the chair arms, his hands, first clasped before him, began to move with his talk, carving figures out of the air. Then one noticed the beauty of his hands, delicately formed with long, tapering fingers, sensitive hands appropriate to a sensitive face. Some time later I was startled to see that face again in a reproduction of a painting by a fifteenth-century painter, Nuno Gonçalves (*circa* 1465). The artist, whose painting is now in the Museu das Janelas Verdes in Lisbon, was seeking to record for the Mosteiro do São Vicente all types and classes of citizens of the realm. In the *Painel dos pescadores,* in the top row, is Salazar—or, without a doubt, one of his ancestors, who were fishermen.

I expressed my surprise at the simplicity and quiet of his office, very different from the west wing of the White House with its hovering reporters, staff coming and going, callers waiting in the anteroom, papers going in and out, and general atmosphere of busy bustle. Our conception of an executive, I said, was a busy man, three telephones on the desk, and that sort of thing. This amused him. He was not an executive, he said. It was difficult to direct things and be busy at the same time. An atmosphere of busy-ness impeded observation, appraisal, and correction. The captain of a ship often seemed the least busy person on it, as he watched everything, made his decisions, and issued his orders. Other people, in the Department of the Presidency, carried out Dr. Salazar's orders. If they did not, he said quietly, almost sadly, they must be replaced.

The metaphor of the sea captain seemed to catch his fancy and lead him on. The successful captain needed abilities of two kinds—ability to keep on his course and knowledge of the sea and seamanship. Shortly after the captain started down the Tagus, bound for Rio de Janeiro, land disappeared astern. He could not see Rio. But with his compass and his knowledge of the sea and of his ship, each day he dealt with the problems of that day, always checking his course, and anticipating, so far as he could, the problems which the morrow might bring. Storms might drive him temporarily from his course. He might be becalmed and drift. But he always watched his compass and his log, guiding his ship onward. One day at a call from the masthead he looked through his glasses. There before him lay the opening between the mountains, beyond which opened the great harbor of Rio.

"When I became Secretary of State," I said, "an older friend said to me, 'Always remember that the future comes one day at a time.' "

This epigram delighted Dr. Salazar. He asked for the Portuguese rights to it. It was the fact of gradualism, he pointed out, which made possible the tasks of those of us who worked at government. It gave us a continuous opportunity to check our course and, with luck, to discover in the developing present some hint of future problems.

With the talk off to a good start, the Ambassador kept it going by leading Dr. Salazar into the economic and political theories of his policies. These he discussed with candor and a wealth of detailed knowledge. No gloss was applied; no effort made toward self-serving statements; no trace of personal ambition appeared. He seemed to me a man absorbed, and relaxedly absorbed, in discussing an endeavor in which he unreservedly believed and yet could observe quite objectively. His talk was spiced with vivid illustration and quiet humor. We both knew, without words, that my agreement or disagreement with his policies was irrelevant. I wanted to understand; he was happy, with a teacher's training, to explain. Time sped by.

When we got on to questions of foreign policy and NATO,

neither Bevin nor Schuman could have been more firmly convinced of the basic importance of the Atlantic community and the measures for its common defense.

Our talk stretched far beyond the time allotted by the Prime Minister's office, but no one intervened to stop us. The Ambassador finally rose, saying that we had trespassed too long. I left knowing that I had never spent a more revealing hour, and had met a man unique in his time, the possessor of a rare mind and even rarer charm. My gratitude to Ted Xanthaky for making our talk transcend the problem of language was great.

I had another glimpse of Dr. Salazar before we left Lisbon. It was toward the end of the conference. We had gone for an afternoon walk in the park in the Castelo de São Jorge. This walled Moorish citadel, set on top of a steep hill in the old east town, the Roman and Moorish town, had been turned into a fort and barracks; its grounds, into a park where everything is white—white flowers, white pigeons and doves and peacocks, a lovely and usually quiet spot. But that particular day was Shrove Tuesday, Mardi Gras, and throughout Lisbon the carnival was coming to its crescendo. The streets were decorated and full of maskers. Amateur, and some professional, acrobats in costumes were parading the streets in pyramids, each narrowing row standing on the shoulders of more sturdy colleagues. Jugglers were doing all manner of stunts. Processions kept passing in elaborate costume. There was much running about with noise-makers, and a goodly number of genial drunks.

The park was largely given over to children revelers in costumes and grotesque masks, chasing one another with balloon clubs, tin horns, and whistles. In the midst of this gay bedlam we came on Dr. Salazar walking with a man who could have been a guard or merely a companion. There seemed to be no other guards about. We stopped to exchange greetings, though they were largely inaudible. While we stood there, children dashed between and around us in flight and pursuit, apparently unconscious of the presence of the "dictator" of Portugal, and certainly in no awe of him. We passed on with a wave, my last glimpse of him as he strolled off being of a tall figure in a swirl of midgets.

In my sketch of Robert Schuman, Foreign Minister of France, 1948–1953, I have told how after the disappointing failures of the NATO conferences of September, 1951, in Ottawa and of December, 1951, in Rome, the Lisbon conference was brought dramatically to a successful finish. At last the collective defense force for Europe under unified command was agreed on and on the way. That it was to meet new difficulties which it would not surmount was still shrouded in the unknown future. As the finish of the conference neared, tension rose, and with it my spirits. In the air I felt the tingle of success, not that flat premonition of deadlock which earlier conferences had given me. I said to the President in one of the personal cables I sent him from time to time, outside the daily official reports, to give him the feel of the situation, that I was betting on a really big success.

When it came we were all elated, and after mutual congratulations and a jovial dinner went to our planes in the early evening. Secretary of Defense Lovett and his assistant, that able and gay Irishman Frank Nash, so soon destined for an early death, were there with the military contingent. Ambassador MacVeagh, on his way home for consultation, Secretary John Snyder, and I were flying back in the President's plane, *Independence,* commanded by a distinguished pilot, Colonel Francis Williams. The Ambassador, generals of the military staff, Portuguese officials, and many of our NATO colleagues came to the airport to give us a tumultuous and happy send-off.

In the midst of the hand-shaking and farewells, Frank Nash shouted to me that he was sending along with us a case of the pleasant Portuguese white wine, pointing to the well-known wicker basket in which it came standing near the plane with our luggage. Others crowding around to speak to me blurred the significance of Frank's answer when, after thanking him, I asked the name of the wine. Some minutes later I awoke with a start to realize that he had said, "Porco de Lisboa." Looking at the basket again I could have sworn that it moved.

"Frank," I demanded, "is there a pig in that basket?"

"Take it easy, now," said Frank, "and look at it this way. The President will come to meet you, hundreds of reporters, television everywhere. There you are, with Lovett and the high brass coming in at the same time. And what are you bringing with you? Bringing home the bacon! Why it's the idea of the year!"

" 'Bringing home the bacon,' my eye! If the press got hold of this," I suggested, "it would end up as 'buying a pig in a poke.' "

But, perhaps, I was wrong and Frank right. For when we had gotten home again and I had told my story to the House Foreign Affairs Committee, Chairman James P. Richards of South Carolina in graphic metaphor said that the American delegation "took time by the forelock and brought home some real bacon," adding as a final metaphoric cherry that Acheson "realized as well as we do that we're not out of the woods yet."

But, to return to the pig in its basket poke, my assistant, Luke Battle, was off like a shot to the plane. There an army Lieutenant was saying mildly to Colonel Williams: "But it's Mr. Nash's orders, Colonel."

"I don't care," roared the Colonel, "whether the Supreme Commander and St. Peter himself gave the orders. No damned pig is coming aboard this plane!" Luke hastened to throw the weight of four Cabinet officers behind the Colonel. The Lieutenant and the basket departed.

The pig, however, did not immediately disappear from the stage. The Lieutenant and his friends, feeling that Frank had exposed them to some humiliation, quietly took the pig to Frank's hotel and put it in his bed. Tired after its exciting evening, it was sleeping soundly when Frank came back to turn in. So completely had the pig adopted hotel life that for some time it eluded all attempts at capture and removal. When finally that was accomplished, only the offer of the pig itself gave the chambermaid heart for the clean-up.

As the *Independence* rose from the runway and soared off to the west, I realized once again that, in Justice Holmes's phrase, I had left "fragments of my fleece . . . on the hedges of life." Lisbon was no longer just a name; the Portuguese, no longer merely the subjects of a king to whom the Pope had apportioned half the world; Salazar, no longer solely a ruler about whom authoritarians and liberals disputed. "I am a part of all that I have met," said Ulysses. From then on some of my fleece was left behind, and some of Portugal came with me.

VI

ARTHUR VANDENBERG AND THE
SENATE

The first time I worked with Senator Arthur H. Vandenberg was fairly early in the course of that change in his outlook on the world which one might call his long day's journey into our times. He had been, to use his own description of himself, one of those "who had been so-called 'isolationists' prior to Pearl Harbor." But "that day," he wrote later, "ended isolationism for any realist." The change in outlook was far advanced by January 10, 1945, when he took the floor of the Senate to urge an international organization with far-reaching powers to revise war settlements and to enforce peace.

This was a long road. Despite his dramatic words about Pearl Harbor—words of hindsight—Vandenberg's change of mind did not come in a sudden flash like that other change on the road to Damascus. I have heard him ascribe it mainly to his work with Secretary Hull and the "Committee of Eight," the special Senate committee on postwar plans. This group met for the first time on April 25, 1944. Here he was thrown, without prior experience or knowledge, into the most involved international problems since the Congress of Vienna. He was to spend the seven years of life which remained to him immersed in these problems. The experience brought out all his many and great talents. It led, too, to a unique service not only to his own country but, ironically enough, to peoples whose affairs and interests he had believed only a short time before to be no concern of his or of his country's.

My first work with the Senator began before the Committee of Eight had been formed. It was in the summer of 1943. Arthur Vandenberg was in a period of deep frustration. He was very much on the outside trying to look in; and he could see nothing. Suspicion consumed him—suspicion, in his own words, of "Executive dictatorship," "by-passing the Senate," "flouting of the Constitution"; suspicion, also, that our Allies were already using for their own ends the victory to which we were contributing so much, and that in doing so they would sow the seeds of another and more terrible war. Nothing is more frustrating than not to know what is going on; and the Republican minority in the Senate had not yet found a channel to the State Department.

His frustration led to a minor and now forgotten tempest in the summer of 1943. It is worth recalling because it hastened the "conversion," as he sometimes called it, of Arthur Vandenberg. The State Department was working on an international agreement, adopted that autumn, to deal with the first and most pressing of postwar problems, the relief and rehabilitation of war-torn countries. Within the Department the task had fallen to me. At length a draft agreement had been prepared with some foreign consultation. Its form on our side was not that of a treaty requiring approval by the Senate, but of an agreement by authority of the President to contribute such funds for relief as the Congress should from time to time authorize and appropriate.

After the draft had been shown to the official leaders of the majority and minority in the Senate and the House, it was published to permit full consideration and discussion. Then the row started. The draft had not been discussed privately with the Senate or House foreign committees or their leaders. This was a mistake—though not so far as the House was concerned, since its rights over appropriations were preserved, and its members had no sympathy with the Senate's prerogatives in treaty making, from which the House was excluded. But in the Senate the publication of the draft set the cat among the pigeons. And it was Vandenberg who indefatigably kept them aflutter. He took the most horrendous view of what he thought was the shape of things to come. The draft he thought "pledged our total resources to whatever illimitable scheme for relief and rehabilitation all around the world our New Deal crystal-gazers might desire to pursue." Congress was to be "confronted with a *'fait accompli'* " and there was to be "no interference with this world-wide prospectus as it might be conceived by Roosevelt, Lehman, Hopkins and Co."

Vandenberg would often be carried away by the hyperbole of his own rotund phrases. My father used to illustrate this very human characteristic by the example of a horse we owned years ago crossing the bridge over the Connecticut River at Middletown. She was gentle and well disposed. But as the buggy began to rumble across the bridge's planking, she would begin to prick up her ears and begin to move faster. More rumble brought more speed, until by the time the Portland shore was reached she was in full gallop and quite a lather. In the same way Vandenberg worked himself up to "a first showdown as to where President Roosevelt's treaty-making power leaves off and that of the Senate begins."

Secretary Hull and I found ourselves in the middle of this "showdown"; that is to say, we found ourselves before a Senate subcommittee appointed to investigate the suspected *coup d'état.* Hull, quite innocent of evil-doing, took umbrage at the vigor of Senator Tom Connally's examination of him and, after the first hearing, withdrew from the pro-

ceedings. It was left to Vandenberg and me to restore peace.
This was not hard to do. As Vandenberg became informed
about the extent of the relief problem and the way it was
proposed to bring all friendly nations into the task of meeting it, he became convinced that the plan was a good one. A
few changes in the text made plain what we had thought
obvious, that the executive could not bind the Congress to
make future appropriations and would seek congressional
authorization. To a critic who thought that the result of all
the fuss was a long way from the projected "showdown,"
Vandenberg replied, "I do not consider this to be the 'surrender'—I consider it to be the 'triumph' of constitutional
procedure."

Well, it was not that, because the issue was never involved.
But, nonetheless, the exercise was a valuable one. It resulted
in Vandenberg's becoming the proponent and eloquent advocate of UNRRA, after having first and publicly exorcised
from it all evil spirits. Without both, it might well never
have been possible. And without this episode, much in our
postwar history might not have been possible. For not only
did this minor experience hasten the education of Arthur
Vandenberg, but it was a forerunner of a ritual of statesmanship that I was to experience many times, and always
with fascination.

Senator Vandenberg, faced with a proposal to take a step
into the strange and frightening postwar world, invariably
began by resisting the proposal. He declared the end un-
attainable, the means harebrained, and the cost staggering,
particularly some mysterious costs which he thought were
bound to occur but which the proposer had not foreseen because of faulty preparation. This first phase, the phase of
opposition, usually lasted through one meeting and sometimes longer. All the while, Vandenberg was testing the

proposal by attacking it; and he was learning a great deal in the process.

Then followed the period of gestation. The proposal grew and developed within him. This period had various manifestations, depending on the time available and the importance of the proposal. It could be, as we have seen with UNRRA, a fairly short time, a time of "assuming for the sake of argument that we go ahead with this, where will it lead and what will it accomplish?" This gave Vandenberg an opportunity to try out statements of the merits of the proposal and possible answers to arguments against it. He thought aloud; and his talk would proceed with mounting enthusiasm as conviction and confidence grew. But this period could take another and longer form, as it did in the case of the Marshall Plan. Senator Vandenberg was Chairman of the Senate Foreign Relations Committee when the Plan was considered in the committee and the Senate. Upon his suggestion, committees were set up under Secretary of Commerce W. Averell Harriman and Julius A. Krug, Secretary of the Interior, to determine the capability of the country to carry out the plan and the economic consequences to it of doing so. This gave time for the country, the Republicans, and the Senator to get used to the idea and for the weight of supporting fact to have its effect.

At this stage Senator Vandenberg was convinced but not committed. Before that occurred, one further step remained to be taken. We called it, variously, "applying the trademark," or "determining the price." This meant either stamping the proposal with a Vandenberg brand, or exacting from the administration a concession which he thought politically important. We have had one illustration in his insistence upon formal changes in the UNRRA draft. Let me give others just preceding the Marshall Plan.

When, in 1947, President Truman was discussing with congressional leaders his proposal for American aid to Greece and Turkey, he stressed that the attacks and pressures upon these countries were not, as surface appearances might suggest, merely due to border rows originating with their neighbors, but were part of a series of Soviet moves, which included stepped-up Communist party activity in Italy, France, and Germany. I can see Senator Vandenberg now, suddenly leaning forward on the sofa in the President's office and saying, "If you will say that to the whole country, I will support you." The presentation was put in this way, to the surprise and disapproval of some commentators.

Again, when the administration bill was introduced into Congress, no mention was made in it of the United Nations. Senator Vandenberg pounced on this and insisted that the bill should provide for cessation of United States aid if and when the United Nations should take charge of the situation. Both he and I knew that this event would never occur, since the Soviet Union would prevent it, but he was quite right in his point. The change was important, and provisions like this have been standard practice ever since. I agreed at once and offered to propose the change at the hearings on the bill. But he would have none of that. The change was proposed as the "Vandenberg Amendment." The brand had been applied; and fair enough it was.

In 1947–48, when the Marshall Plan was in the discussion stage, Senator Vandenberg, remembering the early New Deal, became obsessed with worry that the control of spending the billions of Marshall Plan dollars could give the administration such power as to decide the approaching election of 1948. While he himself had a healthy interest in preventing this, his concern was not due to mere political partisanship. For other Republicans could worry about the same thing and, since they controlled the Eightieth Congress, could doom the

Marshall Plan, which Senator Vandenberg had now come to believe essential. To solve the problem the Senator turned to a plan of organization for administration of the Marshall Plan. The Brookings Institution of Washington was called in to give a detached and expert atmosphere to the deliberations; and finally, an "independent agency" form of organization was worked out, under, but not responding to, the President.

It is no matter that Senator Vandenberg's fears were unfounded. Under both the Truman and Eisenhower administrations, foreign aid has been administered within the regular hierarchy of government without being used for political patronage. The point I am making is that Vandenberg exacted as the price of his support a concession to the opposition which contributed to the acceptance of the proposal—whatever it did to its administration.

This attitude of Vandenberg's and my belief in its importance were to have a curious personal result before the Marshall Plan was fully launched. After the legislation was passed in 1948, the President spoke with me (I was then in private life) about his desire to send my name to the Senate as the administrator created by the act of Congress. I urged upon him, and he reluctantly agreed, that this would be unwise—not because Vandenberg had anything against me, but because, in view of my close relations with the President, the nomination would go a long way, in Vandenberg's mind, toward nullifying his efforts to establish an "independent" agency. This could well be disastrous. The act of Congress was still only an "authorization" for appropriations, a hunting license to go in search of them. The execution of the Marshall Plan still required the appropriation of billions of dollars by a Republican Congress.

The President wisely concluded that here, pre-eminently, was an occasion to seek the "advice and consent of the Senate," which, as a practical matter, meant to consult with

Vandenberg. We speculated as to whom he would recommend, and concluded that it would be Mr. Paul Hoffman, a gentleman of the highest character and ability, wholly acceptable to the President. And so it turned out. Senator Vandenberg never knew what he escaped, but was greatly pleased that his advice had been sought and followed. He became more than ever committed to the support of the European Recovery Plan.

What I have said suggests a strong and practical mind rather than a subtle and original one. Arthur Vandenberg's mind was not original; but it was open. He was not a creator of the ideas which he was eminently capable of receiving and using. A powerful advocate, he was not a great orator. His florid oratorical style, finding its emphasis in hyperbole and often in sheer lung power, had nothing like the range of Churchill's speeches. His importance lies not in brilliance of mind or speech, but—in equal parts—in himself, and in the time and place in which he lived and served. Without Vandenberg in the Senate from 1943 to 1951 the history of the postwar period might have been very different.

When in 1957 a committee of the Senate picked the five most "outstanding" Senators, whose portraits should hang in the Senate reception room, it did not include Vandenberg. The choice fell on Henry Clay, Daniel Webster, John C. Calhoun, Robert M. La Follette, and Robert A. Taft. Yet, in actual accomplishment, a good case can be made that Vandenberg's achievements exceeded those of any of the five, except Henry Clay; and that, as a symbol of his times in the Senate, Vandenberg stands for the emergence of the United States into world power and leadership; as Clay typified the growth of the country; Webster and Calhoun, the great debate of the antebellum days; and Robert M. La Follette, the turbulence of the Progressive Era.

Vandenberg, as I have said, did not furnish the ideas, the

leadership, or the drive to chart the new course or to move the nation into it. But he made the result possible. What was needed was a national consensus, at a time when the hot war which had united the nation was over, and the full consequences of the disruption caused by the war were beginning to appear. How critical was the need can be judged by what happened after Vandenberg's death—I do not say because of it—when the consensus fell apart.

At the end of the war, the opposition of the business community, and its social adjuncts, to the Democratic administration—then in its fourth consecutive term—was ready to break into open revolt; as it did in November, 1946, but without the strength to win in 1948. Meanwhile the times called for action, drastic, unprecedented, and immediate. To those conversant with the situation there was not much doubt about what had to be done. How, by whom, and how soon were the questions. Without Arthur Vandenberg, solutions of these questions could not have been brought into action.

He had, as I have suggested, the capacity to learn and the capacity for action—rare gifts in themselves. As important as either, and giving both scope, he carefully maintained the preconditions for successful action. His prior history of isolationism was an asset which he never allowed to die. His relations with Senator Robert Taft were carefully maintained. Vandenberg's respect for Taft's proprietorship of Republican domestic policy led Taft to respect Vandenberg's position as Republican spokesman on foreign policy, so long as the latter's health and vigor remained. Vandenberg kept the friendship and respect of Senators Millikin of Colorado, Wherry of Nebraska, and Bridges of New Hampshire on the Republican Policy Committee. But, perhaps most important of all, he was in the very heart of the inner circle that ran the Senate.

Its membership did not coincide with the popular idea of importance in the Senate; some were much in the public eye; some were not. They were men of the type and character who, in a quiet way, are apt to dominate any male organization. The main ingredients of such men are force, likableness, and trustworthiness. Alben Barkley, Walter George, and Arthur Vandenberg were, perhaps, the *beaux idéals.* But Warren Austin, Joe Ball, Carl Hatch, Carl Hayden, Lister Hill, Richard Russell, Bob La Follette, Scott Lucas, Burnet Maybank, Bob Wagner, and Wallace White do not exhaust the list of the others. Many of them lunched together, more often than not in the office of Leslie Biffle, whether he was Secretary of the Senate or Secretary of the Minority. Party membership was a comparatively minor consideration. One had to be an adopted member of the group for quite a while to realize that anything was going on under the easy gossip and badinage. Then one discovered that almost everything was going on. The whole business of the Senate was being ordered and, in considerable part, decided.

A word about a few of these men, both in and out of the inner circle, may illuminate Vandenberg's problem in moving policies from hopes to action approved by the Senate. In this alchemy, eloquence on the Senate floor, though important, was not the major ingredient. The real work in shaping a Senator's vote was done off the floor. The height of success, of course, was to make it a favorable one. If that could not be done, a Senator might agree to be absent and unpaired; or, if a majority was pretty well assured, an opponent might be persuaded, while voting against the bill, not to support amendments which might seriously cripple it. Once, when I was Assistant Secretary of State for Congressional Liaison, I wrote a fiery speech against final passage of our bill for an important figure on the other side who agreed to be absent when amendments were considered in the committee and on the floor.

The most implacable opponents of the Truman administration in the Senate, say from 1946 to 1950, prior to Senator McCarthy's emergence from obscurity, were Messrs. Robert Taft and Kenneth Wherry, both high in the Republican leadership. They believed that an opposition should oppose. Since they both totally lacked humor and possessed unlimited energy, their opposition was undiscriminating and ubiquitous. This helped to make it dull, scattered, and less effective than it could have been. Both were singularly obtuse in personal relationships. Bob Taft and I had for many years sat side by side on our university's governing body, the Yale Corporation. The temptation to tease him was too much for my power of resistance. At one meeting he arrived after discussion had already begun and asked me what the subject was. I replied that it was the condition of study and research in the natural sciences at Yale, which, it seemed, required improvement. Taft's critics were given to saying of him that he had an excellent mind until he made it up. However that may be, on this occasion, without a moment's hesitation, he interrupted the speaker by announcing:

"Mr. President, *I* went through Yale without taking a single course in science."

While the Corporation was recovering in complete silence from this remarkable revelation, I was tempted and fell into sin. Addressing the President of the University, I said,

"Your Honor, the prosecution rests." The silence was broken; but the Senator was not amused.

With Wherry, too, I got into trouble. Late one afternoon in 1950 at a private hearing before the Senate Committee on Appropriations, Wherry was badgering me about some minor and dialectical point. He soon began shouting at me across the narrow table. While I was regretting the fate which required me to endure impassively such boring and boorish conduct, I began to wonder when I had last felt the purging sensation of fighting rage. To my horror I could not recall. It was lost in the mists of memory. Then I wondered whether I had lost even the capacity for rage, a chilling thought. So I began trying to work up a temper by murmuring hair-raising imprecations. To my delight I felt the blood rising along the back of my neck and my ears getting hot.

Just then the unhappy Wherry leaned across the table and shook his finger in my face. Without conscious volition on my part I found myself standing, and, in a fair imitation of Wherry's raucous voice, shouting,

"Don't you dare shake your dirty finger in my face!" He bellowed that he would; and he did. A rather inexpertly aimed and executed swing, which I launched at the distinguished Senator from Nebraska, was intercepted by Adrian Fisher, appropriately the Legal Adviser to the Department of State, and a former guard on the Princeton football team, who had accompanied me to the hearing for wholly different purposes. He now enveloped me in a bearlike embrace, murmuring, "Take it easy, Boss; take it easy."

By this time, quite cooled off and rather abashed by my unexpected capacities, I took a look at Senator McKellar of Tennessee, the Chairman of the committee, who was pounding away with his gavel and calling, "Gentlemen, Gentlemen," in a suspiciously choked voice. The secret was told by his ample stomach, which was shaking in uncontrolled glee. When comparative order was restored, Senator McKellar extorted mutual expressions of regret for, and withdrawal of, unparliamentary language from the principals.

The next morning I called on the old Chairman to apologize to him for turning his hearing into a brawl. But, still laughing, he would have none of it.

"No Help from Anybody." Mr. B. Green of the Providence Sunday *Journal* gives a report on the author and the U.S. Senate on March 19, 1950. Published by kind permission of that newspaper.

"Not at all, my boy, not at all," he said, beating his cane on the floor. "Funniest thing I've seen in thirty years on this Hill. I'll never forget Wherry's face when he saw the imperturbable Secretary aiming a haymaker at him. Do you know what I did after you left? I called Harry Truman and told him we could pay off the national debt by putting you two on the vaudeville circuit."

Needless to say, I did not experiment further with my emotions; but curiously enough my relations with Senator Wherry became much easier.

Another experience with Senator McKellar disclosed a coincidence perhaps worth mentioning. Discussions with Senators follow a distinctly Oriental pattern. The subject must not be approached directly and brusquely, but indirectly and leisurely, often by listening to a preliminary discourse by the Senator on how pressed and busy he is. On one occasion, my colleague, the co-Under Secretary of State, and dear friend, Will Clayton of Texas, and I were listening to a long tale by Senator McKellar of his brilliant conduct of a contested will trial in Tennessee a great many years ago. A devastating cross-examination of the widow was approaching its climax. "Then," said the Senator triumphantly, "I sprang the trap with this question," stating it.

Very quietly Will said, "Pardon me, Senator, but you didn't."

After a second of silent incredulity, McKellar burst out, "What the hell do you mean?"

"You see, Senator," Will went on, "I was the court reporter."

From what I have written already it will be plain that the humor of the United States Senate is that American humor of which Henry W. Nevinson wrote in his exquisite *Farewell to America*. The ranks of those who knew and loved Henry Nevinson, the great, gentle, bearded, and terrible-in-wrath British correspondent, are, on both sides of the Atlantic, distressingly thin. As he sailed for home, after his last visit here in 1921, he wrote *Farewell to America*, from which I quote these lines:

> . . . Good-bye to the land where grotesque exaggeration is called humor, and people gape in bewilderment at irony, as a bullock gapes at a dog straying in his field. . . .

> I am going to a land . . . where humor is under-
> statement, and irony is our habitual resource in
> danger or distress. . . . Good-bye, America! I am
> going home.

Another Senator who became a staunch supporter of our
foreign policy and of Vandenberg's efforts was Senator
Charles W. Tobey of New Hampshire. It all happened in a
curious way, which illustrates the intensely personal quality
of judgments and positions taken in the Senate. In selecting
the United States delegation to the International Monetary
Conference, held at Bretton Woods, New Hampshire, in
July, 1944, Henry Morgenthau, Jr., Secretary of the Treasury, wisely wanted a Democrat and a Republican from both
the Senate and House Committees on Banking and Currency, to which would be referred the recommendations of
the conference. By all the time-encrusted rules of congressional propriety these positions were the perquisites of the
chairman and ranking minority member of each committee
and, in event of any declination, went to the next senior member of that party. Secretary Morgenthau, most unwisely, decided to skip Senator Tobey of New Hampshire, the senior
Republican member, because of his isolationist record, and
picked the next ranking Republican. When the Chairman,
Senator Robert Wagner of New York, the father of the present Mayor of New York City, heard of this, he sent for me.

The Secretary's projected step, he told me, threatened to
involve the whole complicated matter of the International
Bank and the International Monetary Fund in a partisan
political row which would go far to dim the chances of successful legislation. Not only would this discrimination strike
at the whole oligarchical structure of Senate committees, in
which every Senator had a present or future vested interest,
but it would be regarded as a particularly mean partisan

attack on Tobey, who was a very decent man even though overinclined to somewhat florid oratory. Tobey was running for re-election within four months, and due to intra-party difference was not yet assured of renomination. To subject him to public humiliation by excluding him from an international meeting to be held with considerable fanfare in his own state would be resented by the whole Senate as a foul blow and might well turn Tobey into a bitter and powerful enemy of the Bank and Fund.

I agreed and undertook to lay the matter before Morgenthau and the President. This was done and the plan was dropped. Since there are few secrets in Washington, thus began a friendship with Charlie Tobey which continued until his death. It even ripened further at Bretton Woods. We had barely arrived at the summer hotel, closed since the outbreak of the war, which was to house the delegates and their meetings, when the Fourth of July was upon us. This would necessitate a ceremony at which someone on behalf of our guests would felicitate and flatter us and a suitable response would be made by an American delegate. While the arrangements were still fluid, my new friend enlisted my help in obtaining for him the assignment to respond, pointing out that the intricacies of international finance were not apt to stampede New Hampshire voters, but that a good rousing Fourth of July speech by their local boy would reach throughout the State, and the nomination would be as good as his.

The Senator little knew how easy it was to gratify his wish. No other American delegate wanted to take the time from exacting homework and lengthy conferences to get up such a speech. So I was soon able to tell him that the honor was his, and felt no compulsion to minimize the undertaking. The speech was a great success and was widely reported throughout New Hampshire. We were soon able to congratulate the Senator on obtaining the renomination of his party.

As the days passed, he progressed from a passive delegate to an energetic, intelligent, and enthusiastic one.

Toward the end of the conference the Senator had one last request to which he attached the greatest importance. Would I do my best, he urged, to persuade Lord and Lady Keynes to come to a dinner which he wished to give for them in his home town, an hour or so away, where he would present to them the local dignitaries, who had never seen, much less met, an English lord. Again the task was not a difficult one. Maynard Keynes understood the political situation very well and knew, at once, that this by no means unpleasant effort would usefully grease the launching ways for his beloved Fund and Bank. But this time I raised the question whether the Senator was not now leading me into disloyalty to my party. It was one thing to be co-operative where the prize was the Republican nomination. But now the prize was the election. What about that? In a moment he had the answer.

"I know what we'll do," he said triumphantly. "I'll ask Democrats, too!" So we settled on that, though it by no means met the point. Lord and Lady Keynes came. The evening was not only a success for Charlie Tobey, but a pleasant one for his guests. I was one of the Democratic guests.

The Senator was re-elected. He proved a tower of strength in securing congressional approval of the Bretton Woods Agreement and United States participation in the Bank and Fund. Two years later, after the war had ended and death had put a new President in the White House, a political overturn and a Republican Congress made Senator Tobey Chairman of the Senate Committee on Banking and Currency. When the new Congress met in 1947, it faced a revolution in American foreign policy, as the nation found itself precipitated into leadership of the non-Communist world in the opening phases of the cold war. The administration found no more loyal and effective supporter than Senator Charles Tobey of New Hampshire. When his isolationist friends chided him for this apostasy, he threw back at them Lincoln's words from his message to Congress of December 1, 1862:

> The dogmas of the quiet past are inadequate to the stormy present. The occasion is piled high with difficulty, and we must rise with the occasion. As our case is new, so we must think anew, and act anew. We must disenthrall ourselves, and then we shall save our country.

Later still, when I was Secretary of State and the McCarthy-Taft attack broke over me, Charlie Tobey never wavered. I feel about this quality of recognizing the imperatives of an obligation as Lord Melbourne did on another subject: "What I like about the Order of the Garter is that there is no damned merit about it."

Even a short account of the postwar Senate would be incomplete without a mention of three giants, Senators Barkley of Kentucky, George of Georgia, and Tom Connally of Texas. Alben Barkley, who left the Senate for the Vice Presidency under Mr. Truman in 1949 and from then to 1953 was known as "The Veep," was not only the most popular man in the Senate, but easily the most popular in Washington. He was warm because he had a deeply affectionate nature and really liked people. In the rare cases where a person precluded even toleration, Barkley's courtesy took over. He was unborable. The problem of bearing fools gladly did not seem to arise for him, as he discovered endless amusement in them. Even a vigorous partisanship gave the impression of a genial and oratorical game which left no scars and led to happy libations in the clubhouse when the game was over.

Barkley's Kentucky audiences expected hyperbole and made their own discount. The heart attack which killed him struck as he declaimed in a political speech his own version of a sentence from the Psalms, "I would rather be a servant in the house of the Lord than sit in the seats of the mighty." The King James version does not stress the undesirability of earthly power but of ungodliness: "I had rather be a door-keeper in the house of my God, than to dwell in the tents of wickedness."*

Warm, outgoing, the center of any group in which he found himself, one of the great raconteurs of his time, his gusto for life was enormous, with no shrinking desire for privacy preventing him from sharing his life. His romance when over seventy with a young and charming widow was followed with almost swooning enthusiasm by the whole country. I remember the Chief Justice of the United States, Fred Vinson, also of Kentucky, remarking at its height, that between Alben's love affair and Pinza's singing "Some Enchanted Evening," Fred could not be sure whether he himself was sixty or sixteen.

Alben Barkley contributed very little to political thought and leadership in the United States. But he did contribute to the means by which that thought and leadership were translated into successful action. He did not belong on the General Staff; he was a good field commander.

Much the same was true of Senator George, except that he seemed to me less admirable in basic human qualities, less kindly, less generous, less outgoing, and more—much more—pompous. Senator George had immense influence. He was, so the phrase went, "a great constitutional lawyer." De Tocqueville has taught us that "scarcely any political question arises in the United States that is not resolved, sooner or later, into a judicial question." This is because all inno-

* Psalm 84, verse 10.

vation in government is challenged in legal action as contravening the Constitution. The Supreme Court is the oracle which, after consulting the omens, gives an answer requiring several decades of further elucidation. "A great constitutional lawyer" is either a judge over a century dead, or a lawyer who interprets the utterances of the Supreme Court as one wishes them interpreted. Since most people who employ the phrase wish them interpreted to prevent innovation, "a great constitutional lawyer" is usually an ultra-conservative. Senator George met this test admirably.

I should say that he had no humor, but rather a regal geniality. He spoke slowly and ponderously, as he sipped a bourbon and water in Leslie Biffle's office before lunch, dispensing the benediction of a sentence here and there. But he was well worth a courtier's assiduous attention. A few days' attendance on him at his home in Vienna, Georgia, could result, as one Assistant Secretary of State played it, in the practical elimination of opposition to and any real debate of the Formosa Treaty and Resolution in 1955. Walter George was a powerful patron and a dangerous opponent.

Fate and temperament made Tom Connally and Arthur Vandenberg collaborators and rivals in the Senate. Since each was a *prima donna,* rivalry often got out of hand, even though they were agreed on fundamentals. Ranking members of their parties on the Committee on Foreign Relations, Connally was its Chairman, except during the Eightieth (Republican) Congress, when Vandenberg took his place from January, 1947, to January, 1949. But whether chairman or not, Vandenberg exercised great power. As I have pointed out, he was the key to indispensable Republican co-operation in obtaining legislative approval and support for policies and programs of the greatest magnitude and novelty.

In effect, sovereignty in the Senate over matters of foreign policy was a condominium; and we in the executive branch had to deal respectfully with both sovereigns. Tom Connally found this irksome, and all the more irksome because he felt that the press, to which he was far from insensitive, accorded Vandenberg an unwarranted and unfair pre-eminence. In a way it was unfair, just as it is unfair that there should be more joy in heaven over one sinner that repenteth than over ninety and nine just persons who need no repentance. Tom Connally shared the quite natural feelings of the prodigal son's elder brother. Connally had served long and faithfully; but the fatted calf was killed, so he thought, for a Johnny-come-lately.

In another way, however, the Senator from Texas contributed to the distasteful comparison. He was a greater debater than Vandenberg, but in a very different style. A master of sarcasm, irony, and ridicule, he would employ gestures and acting to evade the Senate rules and castigate an object of his scorn. "The position now taken by the distinguished Senator," he would say, "adds to his stature"—leaning over and measuring a distance about a foot from the floor—"and gives a true measure of the breadth of his mind"—holding up his hand with thumb and forefinger a quarter of an inch apart. His quick and stinging wit brought laughter and left wounds, all of which would be interspersed through a masterly exposition, or a dissection of the opposing position.

Unfortunately for Connally's public reputation, his appearances on the Senate floor, more often than not, amused the American public, but did not impress it. This public does not agree with Justice Holmes that one need not be heavy to be weighty. We like our public men to be ponderous, platitudinous, and pious, with a strong strain of sentimentality running through all. Vandenberg could exhibit all of these qualities and be a powerful advocate at the same time. Connally would make a noble start along these lines, but the imp of his wit and sense of the ridiculous would always get loose and give the game away. One night years ago at the annual dinner, a gay affair, of a club to which we both belong, I listened with sheer delight to Tom Connally imi- tate himself making a speech in the Senate. No other member of that body could possibly have done such a thing, or even thought of doing it.

Connally took pains to look like the stage version of a Southern Senator—black clothes, the coat cut in a style half- way between a sack coat and a morning coat, black bow string tie, white curls over his collar, a broad-brimmed black hat. Along with these political accoutrements, he adopted a political name. In that *Debrett* of Congress, the *Congres- sional Directory,* he became officially "Tom," not the authen- tic Thomas, just as the late Chief Justice became "Fred," and not Frederic. But the former President is baptismally "Harry," and not Henry S Truman. Furthermore, there is no period after Mr. Truman's middle initial, since it stands for nothing. The explanation, so he told me, is that the middle name was to have honored one of two uncles, each of whose names began with S. At the time of the baptism the issue as to which was the winning uncle had not been re- solved. So the S was put in to be filled out later, as we law- yers say, *nunc pro tunc.* But, somehow or other, his parents never did get the problem settled, so he remains the possessor of an unfilled S.

Dealing with the two senior foreign relations Senators took a good deal of time. Here one had to make haste slowly. The simple thing would have been to talk with them to- gether; but simplicity would have been, if not disastrous, at least hazardous. Connally loved to heckle Vandenberg. Van- denberg when aroused could respond in a way calculated to move Connally another notch toward disagreement for its own sake. So the procedure was first to see them separately, to get each so far committed that only the sheerest wilfulness could undo it. But which to see first? Here was a tricky decision. Both were fairly good about not leaking the content of our talks to the press. But each found it hard to resist leaking the fact of a private talk. Once this was done, the second to be seen knew that he was the second. With Connally this was instant cause for offense. We were members of the same party; he was loyal and proved; yet I turned to his rival first—if, indeed, I had done so. It was to him a poor explanation that Vandenberg was the Chairman of the committee, in the years in which he was.

This problem reached its height in early 1949, when the chairmanship had just changed to Connally and the North Atlantic Treaty was under negotiation. Three times a week, I met in the morning with the Ambassadors of the European countries to hammer out the operative words and in the afternoon with the two Senators to strengthen support among our ultimate partners in treaty-making on the Hill, and not such silent partners either.

Despite all the difficulties and minor pitfalls, the relationship worked. Great things were done; and both men carried the burden in the Senate. To the end of our work together I was able to maintain neutrality in their guerrilla skirmishes. This, I submit, reflects mild credit on all of us.

The characteristics of these men, powers in the Senate, I have said, were force, likableness, and trustworthiness—in varying proportions, as the list suggests. Was Arthur Vandenberg a likable man? Yes, he was. He had humor and warmth and occasional bursts of self-revealing candor. He was not among the "popular" Senators. His ego was too strong for that. Some regarded him, as Mr. James B. Reston of the *New York Times* concedes that he did for a time, as the "most pompous and prejudiced man in the United States Senate." But this was wrong. He was not that; but he took a bit of knowing. When I retired as Under Secretary of State, I wrote to thank him for a warm note which I described as "another of the long list of kindnesses which you have shown me," and "for your outstanding fairness and warm generosity." This was from the heart; he was a good friend.

All these gifts and qualities were what fitted Senator Vandenberg so pre-eminently to perform a service for which the country should be forever grateful: the service of bringing together in support of a foreign policy, dictated by the necessity of events, an administration which could carry it out and an opposition which could have prevented it from doing so. All the brilliance of Calhoun or the eloquence of Webster could not have performed this service. It called for what Arthur Vandenberg had, and was, and had spent a lifetime in acquiring and in being.

I salute his memory with affection and with honor.

VII

GENERAL OF THE ARMY
GEORGE CATLETT MARSHALL

Secretary of State, January, 1947–January, 1949
Secretary of Defense, September, 1950–September, 1951

The moment General Marshall entered a room, everyone in it felt his presence. It was a striking and communicated force. His figure conveyed intensity, which his voice, low, staccato, and incisive, reinforced. It compelled respect. It spread a sense of authority and of calm. There was no military glamour about him and nothing of the martinet. Yet to all of us he was always "General Marshall." The title fitted him as though he had been baptized with it. He always identified himself over the telephone as "General Marshall speaking." It seemed wholly right, too. I should never have dreamed of addressing him as "Mr. Secretary"; and I have never heard anyone but Mrs. Marshall call him "George." The General expected to be treated with respect and to treat others the same way. This was the basis of his relationships.

President Truman has put his finger on another foundation of General Marshall's character. Never, wrote the President, did General Marshall think about himself. This is true and deeply significant. The ego is the ultimate corrupter of man. One who controls it has the strength of ten, for then, truly, his heart is pure. General Marshall's ego never got between him and his task. "If you want to hit a bird on the wing," said Justice Holmes, "you must have all your will in a focus. You must not be thinking about yourself, and, equally, you must not be thinking about your neighbor; you must be living in your eye on that bird. Every achievement is a bird on the wing." General Marshall lived in his eye on the task in hand.

With General Marshall self-control came, as I suppose it always comes, from self-discipline. He was, in a phrase that has quite gone out of use, in command of himself. He could make himself go to bed and go to sleep on the eve of D Day, because his work was done and he must be fresh for the decisions of the day to come. He could put aside the supreme command in Europe in favor of General Eisenhower, because his plain duty was to stay in the Pentagon dealing with that vast complex of forces which, harnessed, meant victory.

My first meeting of any length with General Marshall left an abiding memory of his self-command. It was during the war. We had both gone to Virginia Hot Springs to address meetings of the Business Advisory Council of the Department of Commerce. At the time both Mrs. Marshall and the General's close colleague and friend, Field Marshal Sir John Dill, were seriously ill. But the General, having made the engagement, kept it, and was to fly back to Washington after he spoke. During dinner a note was brought to him. It informed him of the death of Sir John Dill. He spoke unhurriedly for an hour on the military situation, giving with maps an appreciation of the problems and possibilities on all fronts and the resources necessary to exploit them. After a further hour to answer questions, all of which he did without involving security either by way of excuse for not answering or by indiscretion in answering, he went to his plane.

Our first working association gave me an initiation into the General's method of operation. After the Japanese surrender, General Marshall had announced his retirement as Chief of Staff of the Army and, in November, 1945, was pre-

paring to set off with Mrs. Marshall on a long and much-
needed rest, as soon as the Pearl Harbor Investigation, insti-
tuted by the Congress, had concluded its hearings. General
Patrick Hurley, with some asperity, on November 27, resigned as Ambassador to China. That same day the White
House announced that the President had appointed General
Marshall as his special envoy to China with the personal rank
of Ambassador. A good deal later the President told me the
circumstances of the announcement.

Secretary of State Byrnes had come to him with the Hurley
resignation. In very few minutes they concluded that General
Marshall was the ideal man to unravel what Dr. Herbert Feis
has written of as *The China Tangle,** if he could be persuaded
to attempt it. So the President got the General on the telephone, at his quarters at Fort Myer, and asked him to accept
the assignment. Without a question or an instant's hesitation,
General Marshall answered, "Certainly, Mr. President, if you
wish it. When do you want me to start?" "In two weeks," the
President replied. "Very well, sir," said the General and
hung up.

When he next saw the President, General Marshall apolo-
gized for his brusqueness. The reason, he explained, was that
he had heard Mrs. Marshall coming into the house, and since
their vacation together had just collapsed, he needed a few
minutes to put the best face on the new situation.

While the concluding days of the Pearl Harbor hearing
were requiring General Marshall's presence on the Hill, his
instructions for the China mission were being worked out.
Their evolution has been traced in accurate detail by Dr. Feis
in the book to which I have referred. I shall put no gloss on
his account, my interest here being the General's method, not
the content of the instructions. The purpose of his method
was to insure, as far as possible, that the instructions directed

* Princeton University Press, 1953.

a possible and desirable course, that they represented the considered and fully comprehended view of his superiors, and that differences had not been papered over with words designed to obscure meaning.

The operation started with a short paper by the Secretaries of State, War, and Navy—Byrnes, Patterson, and Forrestal—stating what they wanted to accomplish. Then State Department officials, of whom I was one, under the personal direction of Secretary Byrnes, working with army officers under General Hull, representing General Marshall, made progressive drafts of instructions. At length, a draft was reviewed with the President by Secretary Byrnes and General Marshall, and given us for final revision. On December 14, 1945, after Secretary Byrnes had taken off for a Conference of Foreign Ministers in Moscow, leaving me in charge, General Marshall and I went to the White House for the final act. The instructions were read aloud; General Marshall gave his oral restatement of them; the President and I agreed; and the President signed.

Then occurred one of the important episodes of my life. "Mr. President," said General Marshall, "no sensible soldier undertakes a field command without leaving a rear echelon at headquarters. I would like to have one." He went on to explain that out of sight was out of mind, and that the only way to combat this blight was to leave behind a representative who would receive communications from the field, get requests acted upon, and reply within twenty-four hours. This meant a highly placed representative, who could surmount bureaucratic procedure of the sort which let General Gordon be overwhelmed at Khartoum through the glacial ponderousness of overpreparation.

When asked how he wanted this arranged, the General pointed to me. I would be his rear echelon. He would use military communications (the military had its own physical channels) and he would have an officer detailed to bring me his communications, at whatever hour of the day or night they arrived, and to assist me in getting them answered and executed. The President agreed enthusiastically, adding that I was to come to him at any hour for whatever help I needed. The full significance of this arrangement was not slow in dawning on me. Here was, surely, a design for living danger-ously—a special mission, with special communications outside those of the Department, reporting directly to the President through the second in command in the Department of State. Doubtful as I was, even a lively imagination did not forewarn me how tangled my duty and loyalties were to become.

Immediately, however, I was distracted by an unexpected opportunity to serve the much-bedeviled State Department by a bit of comparatively innocent malice. G-5 of the army staff, military government, was under the command of Major General John Hilldring, a protégé of General Marshall's, whom he had saved from forced retirement, when, in com-mand of a combat division, Hilldring had had a heart attack. In a few months we were to be colleagues in the State Depart-ment, where John became an Assistant Secretary. But then he was frustrating many of our cherished plans for the liber-ated areas. John was a vigorous man. We often pointed out to him the waste of facilities when he used a telephone to speak to us from the Pentagon, suggesting that he needed only to open a window and speak in a natural voice. His chief accomplice was an executive officer, one Colonel James Davis, an Iowa lawyer in his civilian incarnation, and an uncom-monly good one. He was a tough opponent and a constant one.

General Marshall and I walked across Executive Avenue from the White House to my office in the old State Depart-ment. "Do you have any officer in mind," he asked, "whom you would like to have detailed to you as liaison with the

Pentagon?" A great light seemed to illumine the whole situation.

"I have, General," I answered, "but I am afraid you can't get him." This idea seemed a novel and puzzling one to him.

"I can't?" he asked incredulously. "Why not?"

"Because," I answered innocently, "he's General Hilldring's executive officer, a Colonel James Davis, and he wouldn't let him go."

"Get me Hilldring," said the General. As he took the telephone, General Marshall sounded more clipped than ever. "Hilldring? General Marshall speaking. Have you an officer named Colonel James Davis in your office?" It was not hard to hear the assent. "Have him detailed to Acheson in the State Department tomorrow." The bellow from the receiver would have split an eardrum if the General had not been expecting it.

"Did you understand me, Hilldring?" asked the General. The answer was apparently satisfactory. The General hung up and left me. After a discreet interval I was not surprised to receive a call from the Pentagon. The views expressed about me were lucid and unfavorable, so much so that I hoped, but did not believe, that John Hilldring smiled as he expressed them. Nevertheless Jim Davis reported for duty the next morning. When many months later General Marshall returned briefly from China and Colonel Davis was about to be released from the Army, both Hilldring and I were summoned to General Marshall's office to hear him read a citation and see an oak leaf cluster added to the Colonel's Legion of Merit.

Throughout 1946 I served as General Marshall's representative—"rear echelon" in his phrase—in Washington and attended him when he returned for a short time in the spring to obtain assurances of loans and grants for the Nationalist government. Already difficulties were mounting for him in

China, but he neither complained nor made any effort to be relieved of his responsibility. He was concerned with doing his duty as best he could. The messages continued to pour in, to be acted upon, and be answered. I was in continuous touch with the President, as Secretary Byrnes was away for the greater part of the summer negotiating in Paris the Italian and satellite peace treaties.

As the summer wore on, both the messages I received and some I sent for the President began to refer to a message brought to General Marshall by General Eisenhower and to various factors which were delaying its execution. One day the President in giving me one of these messages asked whether I knew what they were about. I did not. He then told me that in the spring Secretary Byrnes, for reasons of health, had asked the President to be thinking at his leisure about a successor to the Secretary. This I knew from Secretary Byrnes, who believed that the task would be a difficult one and take time. The President continued that the man he wanted was General Marshall, that he had charged General Eisenhower, then Chief of Staff and about to visit our forces in the Orient, to explain the situation to General Marshall and ask whether he would become Secretary of State when he had done all he could do in China. Eisenhower had reported the General's assurance that he would serve wherever the President directed.

Since President Truman has told all this in his *Memoirs,* it is no longer confidential. When I asked at the time who knew of it, it appeared that he, the two Generals, and I did. Complications in relationships, dimly foreseen in November, were now becoming all too apparent. They did not grow less in the months preceding the change in Secretaries in January, 1947. My best efforts to reconcile my own loyalties left me dissatisfied with the result.

On January 21, 1947, I had returned to my office from the

White House and the ceremony of administering the oath of office to General Marshall, where two years later to the day in the same room I was to take the same oath. Unannounced the General came in. "I will only keep you a minute," he said as I went to meet him. "I want you to stay. Will you?"

Of course I was delighted to serve under him and said so; then ventured the hope that at his convenience we could agree on some future date when I could return to the practice of my profession, from which I had already been absent for six years. He thought this fair and that the time should be fixed then. Would six months be reasonable? That was agreed. Then I asked what he expected of an Under Secretary. There was no established departmental practice. I was to be his chief of staff, he explained, and run the Department, coming to him only when I needed help (and his look indicated that that had better not be often); he wished matters for his decision to come to him through me, and he would issue his instructions through me.

Smiling inwardly at the shock which lay in store for the Department, I explained that the arrangement could not work just as he outlined, and then hastily assured him that I understood what he wanted. Was there anything else?

There was. I have recalled it often because General Marshall's words were so typical of him. "I shall expect of you," he said, "the most complete frankness, particularly about myself. I have no feelings except those I reserve for Mrs. Marshall." With that he left me. The General's statement about his lack of sensitivity was soon to be put to the test.

General Marshall read a speech badly. But he was a master of exposition, without text or notes, of a subject that he knew from end to end. Anyone who heard during the war one of his outlines of the military situation, the strategic plan, with its consequences and requirements, will never forget it. After he became Secretary of State, a few of us whose suggestions and criticisms he had commanded pointed out these truths to him and suggested that he try without text a speech restricted to a single subject, which he would master. The General agreed, chose the Press Club in Washington, and required us to attend as what he called the jury.

As a test of method the speech was a complete failure. As a speech it was a great success. The very enthusiasm and applause of the audience led the General to expand upon subjects he had not intended to discuss until the speech was quite deflected from its original purpose and, though a good speech, did not say what he had intended to say.

The jury assembled in the General's office immediately after the event. In he came, rather glowing from the reception he had had, to see the solemn, disapproving faces. For a few moments, with healthy combativeness, he fought against the verdict; then said that, of course, we were right and that he would read the wretched things in the future, as that seemed the lesser of the evils.

For most men—especially prominent men—a public performance deeply engages their vanity. It is hard to think of Winston Churchill or Franklin Roosevelt asking for or accepting a judgment of subordinates about their speeches. In fact, it would take courage bordering on foolhardiness to venture a criticism to either. But the author of the Marshall Plan wanted it and accepted it. He knew that he must speak carefully and specifically. His job required this. If it involved reading, at which he knew he was not good, he cheerfully accepted the verdict. Who knows or cares, today, whether the audience at Cambridge on that warm June afternoon in 1947 really knew that they had heard the greatest peacetime offer in history and were stirred? But the proposal was clear, and the whole world was stirred when it realized the full magnitude of the Marshall Plan.

General Marshall had the capacity for decision. This is

surely God's rarest gift of mind to man. An amalgam of
mental ruggedness and objectivity (decision and self-analysis
are incompatible), it requires the courage to accept responsibility and to act on information that must always be incomplete. I remember how impatient he became listening to
interminable balancing of "on the one hand" with "on the
other." "Don't fight the problem," he would burst out;
"decide it!"

This reminds me of a remark of Justice Brandeis when, as
his law clerk, I pointed out that a draft opinion of his had
not answered all the arguments of losing counsel. "Some
questions," he said, "can be decided even if not answered."
And the Justice went on to point out that the process of
decision did not require that one view should be accepted as
wholly right and the other view as wholly wrong. It was
enough that the scale of judgment tipped. That was decision.
Thereafter action required one to go forward wholly committed.

The capacity to decide does not necessarily mean the
capacity to decide rightly. But I believe that General Marshall
will be found as the years go on to have been gifted, also, with
that combination of wisdom and intuition which makes for
right decisions.

These gifts were shown in the decisions that led to the
Marshall Plan. The idea, as has been pointed out often, was
the work of many minds. But three decisions of the greatest
importance were made by General Marshall. The first was to
act, and to act immediately. His negotiations with the Russians in early 1947 had convinced him that no agreement
could be reached because they thought that Europe would
disintegrate through economic collapse and that they would
inherit the bankrupt estate. The reports of his staff led him
to believe that this could happen. He concluded that it must
not be permitted to occur. That, to him, meant action at

once. The difficulties in the way might have seemed insuperable to anyone else, but to him they merely called for extra effort.

The second decision was that the plan for European recovery must come from and be devised by the Europeans themselves. The United States should stand ready to furnish the means that Europe could not supply; but it should not, and would not, offer or impose an American plan. Our role would be to help those who energetically and co-operatively helped themselves. The arguments on the other side are easy to imagine. "What, write a blank check?" "Ask others to write the specifications which we must fill?" But the plan never would have succeeded without the decision he made.

The third decision was perhaps the most difficult of all: that the offer should be made to all of Europe and not merely to Western Europe. There was plenty of advice the other way. The Russians, if included, would sabotage the plan. Congress would never appropriate the money. But the General was adamant. If Europe was to be divided more deeply and more lastingly than it was already, Moscow had to do it, not Washington. It was done by Moscow.

Distinguished memoir writers have criticized some of General Marshall's decisions during the war when he was Chief of Staff. Doubtless some of these decisions are subject to criticism. But, as one looks back over the vast congeries of his judgments—involving, as they did, the use of our whole manpower (how much in the Army, how much in production), the development of weapons, the priority of theaters of war, strategy within theaters, the personnel of command—the result, compared with similar judgments in any other war we have fought, is vastly impressive. To Secretary of War Stimson it was more than this. "I have never seen," he said, "a task of such magnitude performed by man." Consider, for instance, General Marshall's selection of officers for high command compared with that of General Halleck in the Civil War. General Marshall knew the army list backwards and forwards and had served with every senior officer on it, and many not so senior. Before the war he had cleared the decks, by a judicious series of retirements. There were no McClellans, Burnsides, Hookers, or Popes among his selections.

General Marshall never answered his critics. It would have been wholly out of character for him to have done so. But, more than this, he had a sort of sympathy with them. His decisions, he said more than once, were adopted and were largely successful. Why should he now try to prove that his critics' views could not have succeeded? If they wished to justify their views, it was their privilege. This tolerance of criticism, this willingness to let the record speak for itself without interpretation by him, is supremely typical of him.

This is not the place, nor am I equipped, to review and defend General Marshall's military decisions—though I am persuaded that it can and will be done most successfully. It is enough here to point out, as Sir Winston Churchill has done, that among the deficiencies of hindsight is that, while we know the consequences of what was done, we do not know the consequences of some other course which was not followed. This need not, of course, blind us to the causes of disaster. But it should make us hesitate to criticize actions which were eminently successful on the ground that some other course might have been even more successful.

General Marshall was dead set against memoirs, autobiography, or diaries—that is, by himself. He refused to criticize others. But his own course was clear and so were his reasons for it. We talked about it many times. He would say, half humorously, that he believed in a division of labor. It fell to some people to be caught up in doing things, in a world of action. Others were qualified to analyze, appraise, and record what had been done.

He was not qualified, he would say, to do this. Perhaps Caesar was, perhaps Churchill was, but he was not. Furthermore, he did not propose to try, because—and these are almost his exact words—however great his responsibilities were, his view was at best incomplete and limited. Some of the factors involved were inevitably hidden from him. Therefore, should he write or speak from the viewpoint of his limited knowledge, his words might be construed by others to be critical of men for whom he had the highest respect and admiration. I wonder how many men have ever had such fundamental humility or so delicate and punctilious a sense of honor.

I must not give the reader the impression of an unbending and stern man. General Marshall could be and often was formidable. But he could also relax when he wished to, and he had humor.

One drizzling Sunday morning during the war the General in his raincoat was sitting on a box pulling weeds out of his Leesburg lawn, when General Bedell Smith arrived from European headquarters. General Marshall told him to go ahead with his report. Meanwhile he went on pulling weeds. When the rain began trickling off General Smith's nose, he burst out, "General, do I have to report standing here in this rain?" "Certainly not," said General Marshall; "turn that pail over and sit on it." But they went into the house.

One of his most engaging traits was his ability to leave any gathering when the time to go arrived. A courteous word to his hostess, or to the chairman, or to the audience, and he was gone like a shot. He had no patience with that insufferable species, the doorway talker, the dallier over departure. When he was through, he was through—and off he went. One of his departures has always seemed to me perfect. Cabinet officers have to have their portraits painted, a process in which the painter often runs afoul of the sitter's self-esteem. For one of his official portraits the General sat patiently many times, courteously responding to all the painter's requests. Finally, the portrait was done. The General said his good-bys and started to leave. "Don't you want to see the portrait, General?" asked the painter. "No, thank you," said the General and left.

General Marshall's recreation was truly recreative and refreshing. He loved to ride a horse, to go bird-shooting, and to work in his garden. There he was always experimenting. One spring he had learned that the Indians used to put fishheads under their hills of corn. So he did, with some complaint from the household and great interest on the part of the neighborhood cats.

As a raconteur General Marshall ranked high, and surprisingly, in view of his official brusqueness and taciturnity, he loved to spin his yarns. At one time when Mrs. Marshall was in the hospital he dined occasionally alone with us. In those evenings he talked about his boyhood in Pennsylvania, his early years in the Army, and people he had known—and delightful talk it was. With a boyhood friend he discovered the law of supply and demand. In the ruins a burned-out barn they set out some tomato plants, and produced the largest, most luscious tomatoes in town, which brought premium prices in the local stores. To their joy, quantity was added to quality. More and more of these delicious giants poured from their vines until they had glutted their market and prices had collapsed.

Then there were the long nights, at the turn of the century, for the First Lieutenant of infantry in command of a lonely outpost in northern Luzon, newly separated from his bride, the first Mrs. Marshall, enduring with a brother officer the interminable tedium between the monthly steamer calls. One evening an idea occurred to him. Over a year or more his wife in almost every letter referred to her weight. She had gained so much, or lost so much. They decided to work out her present weight. Starting with an approximate weight on their departure from the States, Lieutenant Marshall went through the letters calling out the gains and losses, while his colleague kept the tally. In the end they came to the disconcerting conclusion that Mrs. Marshall weighed minus fifteen.

And so it went, until on the stroke of nine o'clock the General made his bow and was gone.

On my last day as Under Secretary of State, June 30, 1947, the General told me that the President wished to discuss some matters with both of us before I left office. We went about noon to the presidential office, where the talk seemed to me curiously inconsequential. Then a sizable group in the rose garden attracted my attention, composed, to my surprise, of my family and friends. At this point the President and the Secretary of State took me out and conferred on me the Award for Merit. No words of approval or disapproval of my service ever passed the General's lips. None were needed.

That day did not, as we both supposed it would, end our work together. A little over three years later the General came back once more on the call of the President to be Secretary of Defense in the hard days of the Korean War. The manner of his coming was again typical of him. The General and Mrs. Marshall were camping with friends in a remote spot in Wisconsin. The White House telephone operator of those days, who was relentless in "getting her man," tracked him down, got the nearest telephone, which was in a country crossroads store, and sent in a message for him to call the White House. The General came out from camp to the store and put in his call at an open telephone surrounded by faithful members of the cracker barrel debating club. The President explained his need; the General agreed monosyllabically and named the day he would report—all to the frustration of the audience.

General Marshall's advent produced a profound change in Washington and in the conditions of my life. Of course, it should have been obvious that in the twentieth century the Defense and the State Departments were dealing with merely different aspects of essentially the same problems—often with identical aspects—and should work in closest collaboration and understanding. But this had never been so. When General Marshall, a former Chief of Staff of the Army, and his Under Secretary, Robert A. Lovett, a former Assistant Secretary of War for Air (before the Department of the Air Force), were Secretary and Under Secretary of State, their personal connections within the Pentagon went far to supply the deficiency. But at the time of the General's return, relations were at their lowest ebb. Within the Pentagon communication with the State Department was permitted only between the two Secretaries and between Deputy Under Secretary of State H. Freeman Matthews and Major General James H. Burns, brought back from retirement for this purpose. This absurd situation would have been even more disastrous than it was had not essential liaison been maintained by illicit secret meetings between personal friends in the two Departments. This state of affairs both contributed to and was solved by the General's and Mr. Lovett's return to the Pentagon.

For the next two years and some months the two Departments functioned as parts of the same government, rather than as two allied but mutually suspicious powers impeded by language difficulties, lack of a common purpose, and representation by inexpert, political ambassadors. The close personal relations which existed between the high command in the two Departments and the fact that the Pentagon command had held the same position in State and had the full confidence of Defense, led to a practice, obvious enough as I state it, but which, I believe, had never happened before and has never happened since (early 1961). General Marshall and I, with some of our highest aides, met as occasion required with the Joint Chiefs of Staff.

In these meetings General Marshall and Mr. Lovett joined the State Department civilians on one side of a long table, while the Joint Chiefs and their aides sat on the other. The General was meticulous in acting as Secretary of Defense and not permitting his status and rank as a five-star general to impinge upon the duties and roles of the men in uniform. This did not mean that he gave the slightest support to the absurd but prevalent notion that problems of our relations with foreign states had "purely military" aspects and "purely political" or "purely economic" aspects which could be separated in the intellectual equivalent of a cream separator. I remember once when General Omar Bradley, Chairman of the Joint Chiefs of Staff, and one of our country's greatest soldiers, started a sentence, "Well, from a purely military point of view . . . ," I interrupted to make a treaty with him that that phrase and its correlative one, "from a purely political or diplomatic point of view," should both be taboo in our meetings.

This leads me to stress another point. General Marshall's great services in civilian posts have often been discussed from the point of view whether it was desirable to have a "military mind" in these positions. Nothing could be more mistaken than to believe that General Marshall's mind was a military mind in the sense that it was dominated by military considerations, that is, considerations relating to the use of force. It is not chance that his name is given to what Sir Winston Churchill has described as "the most unsordid act in history," the Marshall Plan. But more than this, when he thought about military problems, nonmilitary factors played a controlling part. I remember well a talk we had about the strenuous debate during the war between the advocates of the cross-Channel invasion of Hitler's European fortress and the advocates of the Mediterranean invasion through the Balkans, the thrust at the "soft underbelly of Europe," as its chief advocate, Winston Churchill, expressed it. General Marshall did not believe that the southern approach was soft at all. Indeed, he thought that such an operation would greatly increase our casualties.

The principal argument, however, which he stressed in his talk with me, was the increased time involved and the effect of this upon a decision in the Pacific. A cross-Channel invasion would be based upon England, where the forces and supplies were already present. To shift to the Eastern Mediterranean would require a vast amount of additional shipping in the European theater, more troops, and might delay victory in Europe by as much as a year. The consequence could be to stretch out the time for decision in Asia into the congressional elections of 1946. The General spoke of the hazards which inhered in the election of 1864, of that of 1918, and of the great strain of five years of war. All of these considerations militated in his mind against a plan which could add a year to the war in Europe and delay that long the transfer of our power to Asia.

His opponent in the debate, Mr. Churchill, was moved by political considerations, too—the importance of ending hostilities in Europe with our lines as far east as possible. This was an important political consideration. General Marshall's concern was political, too, to reach a decision in Asia before war-weariness might weaken American will. My point is not which political consideration is more valid in the light of knowledge then available, but that the decision in favor of the cross-Channel attack was not the triumph of the "military mind" over political insight.

One further recollection, and a poignant one, throws yet

another light on the character of this noble and generous man. When he returned to the Cabinet in 1950, it seemed natural to all of us that next to the President deference was due to General Marshall. But he would have none of it. The Secretary of State was the senior officer to whom he punctiliously deferred, not only in matters of protocol but in council as well.

While General Marshall's standards for others were severe, for himself they were punishing in the extreme. In the early summer of 1951, after the Senate committees' hearings on the relief of General MacArthur, General Marshall told me that he would shortly remind the President that he had been asked to return to the Cabinet for a year only, to deal with a critical situation. The year would soon be over, and the General would ask to be released. Arguing against this, I produced unexpected irritation. In a few minutes the explanation came. The General was worried about his performance of his duties. Several times in the hearings he had said one name when he meant another. He had increasing difficulty in recalling proper names even when he knew the persons well. He was much humiliated by the weakness. He did not permit himself weaknesses. They did not comport with his duty.

I urged that this inevitable accompaniment of accumulating years was a very minor matter. We all suffered from it; but we still had some good work left in us. He would not listen and insisted on his course. Bob Lovett was an able and worthy successor. But he and all of us, as President Truman has written, sadly missed the strength and wisdom that the General had brought to the government.

I can think of no more fitting words with which to take leave of him than those of the only man I know who could be said to be cast from the same classic mold. On V-E Day

Colonel Henry L. Stimson, Secretary of War, concluding his address to the U.S. high command, said to General Marshall, "I have seen a great many soldiers in my lifetime and you, sir, are the finest soldier I have ever known."

VIII

KONRAD ADENAUER

*Chancellor of the Federal Republic of Germany
Since 1949*

It was during my first meeting with him that Konrad Adenauer tasted the rich wine of wild popular acclaim. In
November, 1949, he was the very new Federal Chancellor,
Bundeskanzler, of the equally new Federal Republic of Germany. Born only a few months before, its capital had been
set up in the sleepy little university town of Bonn on the
Rhine. Both Bonn and Washington thought well of a visit
by the Secretary of State to the new Republic, its President,
Theodor Heuss, a former professor, and its Chancellor, followed by a visit to Berlin newly released from the Russian
blockade. So, after meeting in Paris with the Foreign Ministers of Great Britain and France, described in Chapter I,
I flew on to Frankfurt to stay in near-by Bad Homburg with
High Commissioner John J. McCloy and Mrs. McCloy, both
friends of many years. There I found myself in the middle of
a mystery.

The High Commissioner's residence was a large and comfortable house set in several acres of woodland. Around the
property ran a high wire fence with a single entrance gate.
Fence and gate were guarded by American troops. At night
around the house itself another military patrol circled, while
two German police dogs were turned loose in the woods.
This seemed pretty secure; yet during the night before my

arrival some pheasants, hanging in the tool house attached to the residence, had disappeared. The sergeant major in charge was called in. The competence of the Army was at stake. But the sergeant-major was unperturbed. To the heretical suggestion that the guards might have been playing poker, he calmly answered that surely the dogs were not. Two days later he had the culprit but the pheasants had been eaten.

The dogs, said the sergeant-major, gave the clue. It must have been an inside job, someone they knew. A check at the gate revealed that a handyman who took care of the furnace had gone home carrying a bag of laundry for his wife to do. His house revealed feathers only—and a large family. He was reassigned to a less "sensitive" position, in the jargon of security officers.

From Frankfurt the High Commissioner's train, a diesel, integrated unit comprising an office car, sleeping car, and dining car, very fast and smooth, took us to Bonn. Ten years have now transformed the town I visited that day to a busy, growing government city where a host of new buildings and civil servants jostle and inconvenience the old residents, professors, and students who had made up the small Rhineland community. They were having, I felt sure, the same experience that the residents of Georgetown, Maryland, had more than a century and a half ago when the Father of Our Country put its sprawling, disorderly capital on their doorstep and flooded its quiet, tree-lined streets with the new rulers of the land, diplomats, and camp followers. Now the roar of the evening traffic shakes my poor old house in Georgetown like the ague.

In 1949 Adenauer was by no means the internationally known figure he is today. A vigorous seventy-three, a widower with grown children, his experience had been almost wholly in municipal government in his city of Cologne, where he had first practiced law. He was elected by the city council with the approval of the central government as Deputy Mayor in 1906, Senior Deputy in 1911, and Lord Mayor in 1917, and he continued to serve until the Nazis dismissed him in 1933, and then imprisoned him twice in the next ten years. In 1945 he became one of the founders of the Christian Democratic Union, the Catholic party, from then on taking a growing part in German politics as the opportunity for politics grew from the Advisory Council in the British Zone of Occupation, through membership in Laender, or state bodies, to the interzonal bodies, and, finally, to the Federal Republic.

Adenauer's career had not been rooted in popular appeal. The German *Bürgermeister* of the early years of the century was almost a professional man, who after an apprenticeship often held office for long terms amounting substantially to life appointment. It was in this atmosphere that Adenauer served in Cologne. Then came the decade of eclipse. The years under the occupation were years of political creation— both of the organs of a nation being reborn and of a party system to operate them. His relation to the people was for the most part still ahead of him.

My first and strong impression of the Chancellor—one that has not changed—was of his conservation and prudent use of energy. The control is absolute; not an unnecessary erg is spent on movement, gesture, voice, or facial expression. He moves slowly, gestures sparingly, speaks quietly, smiles briefly, and chuckles rather than laughs when amused. It is not surprising that a man more given to chuckles than laughter is given, too, to irony, rather than broad humor or sparkling wit. An example of the Chancellor's irony has been preserved by Sir Ivone Kirkpatrick, former British High Commissioner in Germany. In a lecture at Trinity College, Dublin, in February, 1957, Sir Ivone said: "My old friend Dr. Adenauer often said to me that God made a great mistake to limit the intelligence of man but not his stupidity."

His whole appearance and manner is of stiffness and inscrutability, enhanced by a hint of the Orient in eyes set wide apart and a flatness of the bridge of his nose—a pure coincidence since it has no basis in ancestry. But a first sense of cold aloofness goes, if, after due deliberation, he gives his confidence and friendship. This he has done most generously with me. I know no more delightful and uninhibited companion in a good gossip. And no more considerate friend. When one has left office, those who have continued on become easily and understandably absorbed in new connections. But the Chancellor—in Bonn or Washington—always has the time and desire for talk with old friends.

That November morning he was getting to know me, but under McCloy's genial and high-spirited prodding he began to move toward an easier give and take. Necessarily we talked a good deal about the immediate future and its problems, but in recalling the more general talk which followed I am struck by how much of his later policy was forecast. Adenauer, the good European, came out in some sentences indelibly impressed on my mind.

"Germany," he said, "is in some ways just the opposite of your own country. Your rivers run from north to south. In your early days they came from the unknown bearing nothing but water. Our rivers flow from south to north, and in our early days they brought us, here in the Rhineland, civilization and Christianity. We belong to a continent in a way you do not." This opened fascinating paths which we eagerly followed toward the idea of a developing unity of Western Europe through the enduring reconciliation of France and Germany. A German proverb declared, he said, that Germans take on the color of the wall, tend to conform to their environment. Probably this was true of most people, he went on, except—with a twinkle—the English, among whom eccentricity is much admired. At any rate, it was not good for people to become isolated. It accentuated their least desirable characteristics. Germans, like other Europeans, would profit by escaping from a purely national environment into a wider one in which their more liberal traditions would find strength through companionship.

We spoke of the future unification of Germany, a prospect which then caused so much apprehension among her continental neighbors. The Chancellor, again stressing the theme of European unity, pointed out that the apprehension was directed toward the revival of the nationalist, militarist Germany which had twice sought to impose its will upon Europe. But the idea of the Germans' uniting with their European neighbors within a still wider Atlantic association should raise not apprehension but hope of a new day.

Our talk gave me hope of one. Here was a man, I thought, whose mind—once the yeast of reconciliation began to work in France and Germany—could travel the road along which all our measures for the recovery and security of Europe had been moving.

After lunch with Dr. Adenauer and his Cabinet in a small private room in a very Victorian Bonn hotel, where we drank the delicious white wines of the Rhineland and made formal speeches, I went off to meet the leaders of the opposition in the Bundestag, the Social Democratic party. Two of them, the two lieutenants, were pleasant men, Erich Ollenhauer and Carlo Schmid. But the leader, Kurt Schumacher, was a bitter and violent man. Crippled, so I was told, by tortures inflicted by the Nazis, a leg and arm were of no use to him, and he moved about supported by a statuesque and shapely blonde. She lent a distinctly bizarre note to an otherwise somber composition.

Schumacher at once launched into an unrestrained and

bitter attack against Adenauer, whom he apparently hated, on the strange ground that Adenauer was working smoothly with the British, American, and French occupation authorities. I pointed out what immense benefits this had brought to the German people and wondered what sensible alternative he thought possible. Apparently the Russians were to be induced to reunite Eastern and Western Germany by a German policy of aloofness to the West, which almost ten years later became known as "disengagement"—the removal of all foreign troops from the soil of a "neutralized" Germany. The clear demonstration in the Paris Conference of Foreign Ministers during the preceding May that the Soviet Union was not prepared to make any agreement about Germany which would weaken Soviet control in the Eastern Zone was immaterial to him.

Breaking off this futile interview as soon as politeness permitted, I went on to a reception which the Chancellor was giving for me to meet the Bonn government officials and the diplomatic and American communities and then, accompanied by Dr. Adenauer, to the High Commissioner's train. By this time the North European winter evening had fallen and the street lights were on. Surrounded by motorcycle police, in white coats and helmets, our motorcade sped through empty streets to the square before the railroad station. To my surprise it was packed with people held back by police lines to make a passage for us. Through this we went in closed and darkened limousines through the station itself and onto the platform alongside our train.

This, I protested to Adenauer, was a very poor way to do things. The crowd had waited most patiently to see the Chancellor and his visitor, and all they had seen were some closed black limousines speed by. He and I, alone, I proposed, should walk out into the square, shake hands, and walk back. The security officers had tantrums; Dr. Adenauer agreed. So out we went. We got pretty nearly to the center of the ill-lighted square before word got through the crowd what was going on. Then cheering broke out and the police lines bulged as those behind pressed forward to get a look. When we stopped and shook hands, everything exploded. The police lines broke; we were picked up and carried to our train, with as many as could push into the station following.

At the train all semblance of order disappeared. Our colleagues were inside, or rapidly got there. The doors were closed. Dr. Adenauer and I were rescued and put aboard, where we lowered a large window and continued to wave and shake hands with one another and with members of the crowd on the platform. Boys held up papers to be auto-graphed, climbed on top of the train, and tried to get into the engine. After half an hour of bedlam, the Chancellor was maneuvered back into his car, and escorted out of the station by a cheering crowd. We pulled slowly into the yards, where railroad men scraped off boys and assorted stowaways. As we finally started on our homeward way, we all agreed that, while we had fouled up the protocol of the departure, we had introduced a desirable element of democratic disorder into the political life of the Federal Republic. And Adenauer had had a popular triumph.

The near miracle of the German Federal Republic under Dr. Adenauer's Chancellorship was made possible by the work of the two great American proconsuls, General Lucius D. Clay, Military Governor of the American Zone in Germany, 1947–1949, and John J. McCloy, American High Commissioner to Germany, 1949–1952.

A common and specious maxim is that what our soldiers win on the battlefield our diplomats lose at the conference table. This assumes that what is won by force is solid and lasting, that it will remain unless lost by mismanagement. Nothing could be more false. What is won by force is as transient as the colors of a sunset. Force, at most, destroys opposing force and leaves the loser defenseless. At once, almost within the hour, a wholly new situation arises. Only two courses are possible. Force can continue to be applied as the means by which the victor attempts to rule directly or by local agents. The defeated then become a subject people; resistance to the victor's will is crushed by force, as it was in Hungary.

The other course is based not on coercion but on enlisting the consent of the defeated in policies mutually beneficial to victor and vanquished. In our time a truly democratic and civilized society cannot long continue coercion of a vanquished people. Their own consciences rebel, as the British public rebelled against coercion by the Black and Tans in Ireland after World War I and as the French are today turning against coercion in Algeria. In totalitarian countries the people do not know what their government is doing elsewhere, and they are coerced themselves.

What the allied soldiers won in Germany was the defeat and destruction of Nazi arms and government and an opportunity for a fresh start. It was soon clear that in Russian-controlled Germany the new start would consist of sovietizing the Zone under the guns of the Red Army. In the Western Zones the very nature of the conquerors dictated, as I have suggested, a radically different course. There would be coercion, to be sure, of the remnants of the Nazis. But the main task was infinitely greater, and the time given was short. It was nothing less than pushing, persuading, inspiring the Germans to rejoin Western civilization and the community of Europe. This required emancipation from a century of German thought and from the preceding decade's pagan and bestial debauch under National Socialism.

This was the task that General Clay assumed, and only a man of his iron will and colossal stubbornness could have done so. Germany had collapsed, utterly and completely. With Hitler's suicide and the Army's surrender, the whole political, social, and economic structure fell in on a people exhausted, bewildered, morally numb, without self-respect or faith in anything, without even resentment. With everything to do, Lucius Clay did everything. We watched the resurrection of a nation under his evoking will. This is no place to describe it; only to salute it. But one achievement coming toward the end of his governorship must be mentioned. After laborious foundations had been laid restoring will and sense of direction to the people, establishing the fundamentals of social life, clearing away the worst of the physical destruction, it was essential to lay a basis for a recovery of production. The people were ready to work for it; but the financial and monetary system of Germany was in ruins; its money worth almost nothing. Work and the desire to work were only frustrated by this chaos.

A proconsul, possessing all power, and like General Clay not at all averse to using it, can do things which only the bravest leaders in a democracy, like Camille Gutt, Finance Minister of Belgium during World War II and until 1945, dare to attempt. On June 20, 1948, General Clay carried out the currency reform of Western Germany. This was the starting point of German recovery. By the middle of 1957, the *Deutsche Mark* had become the strongest currency of Europe. With the great lift of the Marshall Plan, added to the establishment of a sound currency and financial institutions, the German economy staged a truly spectacular recovery. West Germany ranked again among the world's industrial leaders. This gigantic stride from the ruin and collapse of 1945 took place within a little over a decade.

McCloy's tenure saw the establishment of a democratic government in Germany and its movement to virtual sovereignty. His task was not greater but more subtle than Clay's, for just as the Military Governor gave way to the High Commissioner, so he in turn was replaced by the Ambassador. McCloy largely bridged and made possible the last transformation. The transfer of power is hard enough under the best conditions. We have learned in well-established societies that the more abrupt it is the better. "The King is dead; long live the King" is best. Regencies are difficult. In this country we have cut down our interregnum from four months to a little over two. In Britain it takes a few hours. But with the Federal Republic the process lengthened over several years. Institutions had to develop sinews, confidence had to be developed and security provided; for here the transfer was from three sovereigns—with a fourth making all the difficulties which perverse ingenuity could devise.

In building confidence which alone could bring a new unity to a European community containing the German people, the doubts and hesitations were not all on one side. I remember well in the autumn of 1951, when plans for the European Defense Community had progressed to the point where it was becoming urgent to change the three-power relations with Germany from occupation to alliance, Dr. Adenauer for the first time was invited to meet, in Paris, with the French, British, and United States Foreign Ministers. He asked for a meeting at the end of our first morning session with Ambassador Bruce, Mr. McCloy, and me. After a lunch at the Embassy, given by Ambassador Bruce, we met in privacy. The Chancellor said that the Federal Republic was on the brink of far-reaching decisions. In making them, a major factor must be his judgment of the future course of the United States. He knew Europe and could make his own appraisal of his fellow Europeans. But the United States was and long had been more of an enigma. His countrymen had twice misjudged our intentions. A third misjudgment could be fatal.

Germany, he went on, if she entered a European defense plan, and if one took a cynical point of view, could be fattening herself to make a more acceptable sacrifice in a future arrangement with the Russians. He would like to put a blunt question in the hope of getting a blunt reply: Was the United States as deeply committed to the defense of Europe as it was asking the Federal Republic to become? He hoped that we would not take offense at his frankness. I said that the question was a proper and natural one. As far as the government under Truman was concerned, the answer was that we were even more deeply committed. I thought that the same was true for whoever followed us, whatever the political complexion of the government. Even Senator Taft would find that forces far stronger than the tradition of isolation compelled common cause with Western Europe. Beyond that I could not see. The effect of unknown developments in technology, the problems of maintaining a coalition against the centrifugal force of parochial interests were beyond prediction. But there was no hope for any of us if the alliance fell apart. We could not guarantee it. It was up to all of us, to him not least, to make it work. The Chancellor said he was satisfied; we went back to work.

In the work we faced, in meeting the never-ending difficulties which arose, the characters of Adenauer and McCloy and the relationship between them was indispensable. McCloy has that most priceless gift, vitality, and the force that goes with it. To this are added ability, judgment, and good nature—an expansive, happy nature with no littleness, suspicion, or jealousy about it. He was well served in the field, helped and supported in Washington. He and Adenauer got on. Neither one was strong on tact, but they dealt frankly and forthrightly with each other. They prodded the lagging processes of liquidating the occupation and set a firm course which gave confidence. An occupation is a wasting asset, like any administration—only more so, because it is foreign. The opposition to those in power, which always grows in a free society, grows faster when they are foreign conquerors. So whatever is to be done should, as Macbeth observed in another connection, be done quickly.

McCloy's service was not only in the wisdom of his guidance and co-operation with the Chancellor and the German people but in the speed with which he was able to liquidate a tripartite occupation—no simple matter. Experts can argue for years over thousands of issues, and showed every disposition to do so. We set as a target May, 1952, to end all this. To my delight, McCloy and Dr. Adenauer adopted the historic method of dealing with filibusters—night sessions. Their British and French colleagues—and some Americans—could not stand the pace. Reason would take command and speech falter as dawn began to break and, with it, the horror of resumption at ten o'clock the same morning. Agreements came fast then; and the Chancellor, *"der Alte"*—"the Old Man"—remained as fresh as ever.

I have told in my sketch of Robert Schuman (Chapter II) how we achieved our goal and reached agreement in May, 1952, ending the occupation. On the evening before the final ceremonies, and when a few issues were awaiting French agreement, the Chancellor gave a dinner for the three delegations and their ladies in his official residence, the Palais Schaumburg in Bonn. Set in spacious grounds running down to the Rhine, it had across the back a broad and balustrated stone terrace, whose steps gave onto the lawn.

After dinner and coffee we moved onto the terrace. The evening was warm; the freshness of spring around us; a new moon hung above the trees. Couples sat or walked about the terrace. A German singing society gave us exquisite harmony at the bottom of the steps. My wife pressed my arm.

"Watch this," she said, looking across the terrace and then to the door, "The Student Prince, Act II." The French Foreign Minister, M. Robert Schuman, was standing talking with a small group. One of his smoothest aides had come out of the palace and was looking about him. When the aide spotted his Minister, in the lyrics of *My Fair Lady,* he "oiled around the floor," with elaborate casualness, a greeting here, a bow there. The Minister turned anxiously for a hurried conversation, and then back to his group.

"Do you bet Anthony or I come next?" I asked. She chose Anthony Eden, and won. Again the gliding motion, so purposeful in its indirection, took him to Mr. Eden. He talked while looking at the moon and apparently about it.

"Let's join a group and make it harder," I suggested as Eden gave a nod and the aide looked around for the third man. We did so and were well involved when he sauntered up. My wife entangled him in a web of conversation, frustrating every attempt to escape by wrapping a new and sticky thread around him. But the scenario clearly called for a talk between us, so I became actor again, intervened in her sadistic game, and let him edge me away from the group.

Paris, he said, had accepted a compromise worked out that afternoon with a modifying proviso. Mr. Eden would agree if I would. M. Schuman urged that I should. I did. The agreement was complete. One phase of a great work had come to fruition in a comic opera setting. I walked over to have a glass of champagne with Adenauer.

Like Sir Winston Churchill, the Chancellor, while a shrewd politician, has a sense of acting in the stream of history. This gives perspective to his thought and continuity to his action. The qualities which arouse his admiration and confidence are decisiveness, resolution, and strength. He distrusts facility. "There is such a thing as being too clever," he said to me of a well-known public figure. Blunt talk is best to find out where one stands and what another means to do. If phrased courteously, as is the Chancellor's custom, it is the best diplomatic method. A "diplomatic" statement should be one which combines precision with courtesy and persuasion.

To work with the Chancellor was among the satisfactions of my experience. I have never known him to hesitate or hedge in carrying out his word to the last letter. On the contrary, he has been merciless to subordinates of whose tendency to trim his commitments I had occasion to complain. His perspective and sense of history I see before me in a note from him written in January, 1953, when we were parting officially. He described the work in which we had joined as in the pursuit of a security system for free nations, and of a genuine community of Europe to assure peace and the development of Europe's economic resources and her great cultural values. He wrote, too, of the difficulties still in the way with which he would continue to wrestle. In the part which he was good enough to think I had played in bringing our generation within reach of a goal so long only a dream to those who had gone before us, he found no small basis for a place in history.

The letter was like him in its thought and its generosity. In sending him my deep appreciation and warm thanks, I spoke of his patience through the hard years, his reasonableness under trying circumstances, and his steadfastness of purpose through all. From the sidelines I wished him Godspeed as he pressed on with the task.

IX

A STATE VISIT: VIENNA, 1952

By June, 1952, the Austrian people had had a long diet of frustration. It had begun in 1914, but the last phase dated from the end of the Second World War. One would have thought it obvious enough that the Austrians had been dragged into the war chained to Hitler's chariot. But this view did not suit the Soviet book. There it was written with vindictive and specious logic that Austria was not a victim but an enemy. Hence, Soviet reasoning ran, that unhappy country must be made to pay in a way to fasten Soviet control on her people for generations to come. The Council of Foreign Ministers gave up their effort to write an Austrian peace treaty at the London conference of November, 1947, and turned the task over to deputies. As I have recalled (Chapter I), another attempt by the Ministers in May, 1949, was also blocked. By June, 1952, "despite several hundred meetings of the representatives of the four powers," as a State Department note sadly put it, there was still no agreement on a treaty and the occupation still continued.

In 1955 the Soviet attitude was to change overnight; and the change would not be due to any negotiating by the Western powers. When in February, 1955, the Soviet government opened direct talks with Chancellor Raab of Austria, it was motivated not by Austrian considerations but by concern over Western Germany. Chancellor Adenauer was moving steadily in discussions with the NATO powers toward

becoming a member of that alliance and playing an important military role in it. The Kremlin, determined to prevent this if possible, decided to give the Germans an object
lesson that the best approach to the unification of Germany
and the end of the occupation of East Germany would be to
pay the price which the Austrians have to pay—stay clear of
alliances with the West and take a position of neutrality.

Both sides moved fast. On April 15 an Austrian-Soviet
communiqué announced that their talks had ended in agreement and that they were ready to sign a peace treaty to which
the West would be parties. However, the agreements with
West Germany ending the occupation and admitting Germany to NATO became effective May 5 and May 6.

The signature of the Austrian treaty took place ten days
later. It was the result of the action of the West toward
Germany, not of negotiation about Austria—the very sort of
calculation to which Sir William Hayter referred (see page
105) as the only effective stimulation to Soviet action, a calculation of their own interest or necessity.

The events of 1955 were not foreseeable in 1952 and the
Austrians understandably were discouraged. But they were
unbowed. Their spirit never drooped, nor did their ingenuity in circumventing the Russians. They had one great
advantage over other Russian-occupied lands. The Soviet
government had not established a Communist regime in the
Russian Zone of Austria; the Austrian government's writ ran
throughout the country, though its power to enforce it did
not always do the same. This Soviet decision ultimately saved
Austria from communization and partition.

We had no doubt that the Austrians fully understood the
deep concern for them which was felt in the United States.
The presence of our troops in their country, the support of
the Austrian people and the rehabilitation of the Austrian
economy through the Marshall Plan, such acts of personal

understanding as private American help in the rebuilding of St. Stephan's Cathedral and the Vienna Opera House—all gave eloquent testimony to that concern. They knew, too, who was responsible for the long stalemate in ending the occupation. But often a more simple outward and visible sign of friendship is useful.

The most easily understood symbol of one country in another is a person. So, from the beginning of human history, the state visit has been the means by which one country through its government expresses its friendship to another. This is not the sole use to which state visits have been put. Another purpose has been dramatized for us by the writer of the Book of Kings.

> And when the queen of Sheba heard of the fame of Solomon . . . she came to prove him with hard questions. . . . Solomon told her all her questions: there was not any thing hid from the king, which he told her not. And when the queen of Sheba had seen all Solomon's wisdom, and the house that he had built, and the meat of his table . . . and the attendance of his ministers . . . there was no more spirit in her. And she said to the king, It was a true report that I heard in mine own land of thy acts and of thy wisdom. Howbeit I believed not the words, until I came, and mine eyes had seen it: and, behold, the half was not told me: thy wisdom and prosperity exceedeth the fame which I heard.

The Queen's visit was an intelligence mission. When she found that fact surpassed rumor, she adjusted policy accordingly. In part, Mr. Khrushchev's state visit to the United States in 1959 was for the same purpose. He came to see whether the reports he had heard in his own land were true and to prove us with hard questions. We would like to believe that after "the attendance of [our] ministers" Mr. Khrushchev was so impressed that "there was no more spirit" in him. But, alas, the record will not give us that comfort. On the contrary, his performances at the Paris Summit Meeting of 1960 and at the United Nations General Assembly in the autumn of that same year are pretty clear proof that the impressions he received made him even bolder and more arrogant.

But, in part, Mr. Khrushchev had another purpose which had its analogue in another state visit. In 1898 Kaiser Wilhelm II, after visiting Sultan Abdul Hamid, went on to the Holy Land. From Haifa to Jerusalem he moved in ostentatious grandeur, escorted by an array of Ottoman officials and a regiment of soldiers. Thomas Cook had provided this bizarre crusade with a city of tents, including six for receptions, and an army of servants. "The Kaiser," writes Joan Haslip, "entered Jerusalem dressed in shining armour, in memory of the Crusader knights, but the white silk coat which protected him from the dust was fashioned with a pilgrim's cowl and he impressed the crowds with his piety by getting off his horse as soon as he reached the outskirts of the city and kneeling down to say his prayers in the middle of a dusty road."*

Prince von Bülow, who was a member of the party, shows us in his memoirs a photograph of the Kaiser mounted and in raiment white and glistering, against the background of the tent city. He describes his sovereign as wearing "over the gorgeous gala uniform of the Gardes-du-Corps a very artistic silk mantle, interwoven with gold threads, which Fraülein von Beaulieu, the Empress's chief waiting woman, had secretly embroidered for him."† Even in the photograph, it is an impressive sight, as it was intended to be. The whole

*Joan Haslip, *The Sultan* (Cassell, London, 1958), p. 241.
† Prince von Bülow, *Memoirs* (Little, Brown, Boston, 1931), pp. 296–97.

purpose of the visit was to impress. The Kaiser was angling for the concession of the eastern half of the Berlin-to-Bagdad railway, which he obtained a year later, and wanted to bring home to the Sultan that German friendship was worth the price of the concession.

Mr. Khrushchev, too, wanted to impress, but for a different reason. He wanted to impress upon the American people and their government that if he got his way he could be quite a jolly fellow; but if he was crossed anything might happen. He delighted in showing his unpredictable, powerful, irascible temper. He flew into tantrums. He became the personification of a dangerous power, possessed of nuclear weapons and vast military forces, which one crossed at one's peril. This latter impression was made too successfully. It was so overdone that, in some quarters, at least, it ended the illusion that our power was adequate for all emergencies and revived the determination to make it so.

Our purpose in June, 1952, was the simpler and more usual one I mentioned first. We believed that a state visit would be a symbol to the people of Austria in their time of discouragement of the deep interest in them and desire to help them through their troubles which was felt in this country. The Austrian Chancellor, Herr Leopold Figl, had visited the United States in May, 1952. But no American Secretary of State had ever paid a visit to Austria. We inquired whether a visit would be welcomed; and found that indeed it would be. Not long afterward the President's airplane, the *Independence,* was on its way to Vienna.

On our way we had stopped in Berlin to fulfill a promise I had made to lay the cornerstone of the American Memorial Library. This was a colorful ceremony. The workmen building the library attended in the ceremonial dress of their various guilds; the Mayors of the city, the Commandants of the Western powers, and a great host of citizens filled the grounds around the library and spilled over into the street. A block away beyond the elevated railway lay the Soviet Sector. I was told that a good number of East Berliners were in the crowd. When the mortar was spread and the stone containing a box of papers lowered into place, the master mason handed me his hammer and, having been carefully coached, I tapped the stone with it and spoke a wish for the building yet to be. Others followed, each with a wish, like fairy godmothers around a cradle. We must be careful, so we were told, not to tap too hard. A lusty blow by Mrs. McCloy had on one occasion cracked a stone.

Of another hazard we were happily ignorant. Some time later in the course of excavation on the spot where I stood to make my speech, the diggers unearthed an unexploded bomb dropped on Berlin during the war, and a good-sized one, too. A demolition squad removed it without mishap. Had I known what was so close under my feet, I doubt whether I should have detained my audience so long.

Six years later I visited the library again, completed and in full operation. It had been both beautifully and functionally designed, a combination not always easy to achieve. The children's wing with furniture to scale and murals and gardens for them, as well as study rooms, was something I had not seen anywhere else. As we walked through it, the library was full of people, many of them East Berliners, with busy groups around the desks noting books borrowed. I felt happy to have had a part at the baptism of so fine and vigorous an institution.

When we touched down at Tulln Air Base, the American airport twenty miles from Vienna in the Soviet Zone of Occupation, we were greeted by the Foreign Minister Karl Gruber and Frau Gruber and the American Ambassador and High Commissioner Walter Donnelly and Mrs. Donnelly. After reviewing the guard of honor and meeting the press, a two-car train with a glass compartment at the back took us to Vienna. Rarely has so short a trip been so interesting.

A beautiful June Sunday had filled the countryside with picnickers, who gave us friendly waves. In the towns and railway stations the tracks were lined with gay crowds, throwing flowers and cheering. Behind them were groups of Soviet soldiers who turned their backs as we passed. This was repeated, obviously on orders, by others on flatcars with Soviet military equipment. But the people paid no attention to them whatever, going on with their greetings as though this somber and sullen enemy presence did not exist. On barns and walls along the railway "Ami go home" had been splashed in whitewash; but everywhere "go home" had been crossed out and "staye [sic] here" painted over it by those of contrary mind.

An hour's slow run brought us to the Vienna railway station, where after being greeted by Chancellor Leopold Figl and Vice Chancellor Adolf Schaerf we walked to the plaza beyond the station to review an honor guard of Austrian gendarmery and waved to a large and cheering crowd of Viennese. On the way to the High Commissioner's residence we stopped for another review—and a most thrilling one—of the 796th Military Police Battalion of the United States occupation force in their headquarters in the large courtyard at Stiftskaserne. Never have I heard "The Star-Spangled Banner" played as it was that day; shivers went up and down one's spine. Usually it is played too slowly, solemnly, and even mournfully, with quavering soprano notes, at the three-quarter mark. But the band of the 796th Battalion had different ideas. With verve, power, and a brisk pulse every note became an assertion with no nonsense about it, giving to a tune which can easily become sedate all the belligerency of the *"Marseillaise"* at its best.

Nothing could have better portrayed the spirit of General

Fitts's command, efficient, proud of their service, impeccably turned out in paratroopers' uniforms with white cap tops and chin straps, white gloves, white rifle slings, and white laces in their high boots. They patrolled Vienna in the white automobiles of the combined Vienna security force with the flags of the four occupying powers painted on the outside, and inside, a Russian, British, French, and American military police soldier, to see that law was enforced as well as order. This made a vast difference from the situation in East Berlin, where there was order aplenty, but where, in a famous phrase, law was found at the end of a policeman's stick.

Our first real taste of Vienna came later when Chancellor Figl presented us with an evening of unadulterated delight. Figl is the personification of a gay and mischievous fox, with many of the qualities generally attributed to a lion. The son of a peasant family and head of the People's party, he became Chancellor to preside over a coalition government. Shiftings of parliamentary strength later moved him from head of government to Minister of Foreign Affairs. As I write, he is President of the Austrian Parliament. Leopold Figl is a short and slim man, of quick movements. Hair and close-cropped mustache are—or were in 1952—reddish; nose short and pointed; eyes intelligent and humorous behind colorless rimmed spectacles—all give him an alert, eager air.

He was alert, too, in preserving the integrity of Austria. This involved insistence on freedom of movement, commerce, political activity, and a common currency within the whole country. The Russians were continually attempting to treat their Zone of Occupation as a separate entity. The matter of passes was an instance of this, in which the Chancellor gave a personal lead. His birthplace, where his mother lived, was in the Soviet Zone. The Russians, at the outset of the occupation, gave him a pass to present at the check point on the border of the Soviet Zone. He promptly

tore it up, announcing that the Chancellor of Austria did not
need permission from anyone to go anywhere in Austria.
This produced a palaver at the check point, delaying, to be
sure, but giving Figl great pleasure. In time he was allowed
to go on his way. Soon a new pass was sent to him, and
immediately torn up. In the end the Russians gave up. The
same thing happened when they told him not to hold political
rallies on these visits. He always did.

As soon as he knew the date of our arrival, he began to
plan. In June the concert and opera season was over. But the
Chancellor explained the situation to the management,
players, and artists, with the result that they all came back
from their various summer pursuits to put on for us Mozart's
The Marriage of Figaro. And not only to perform it, but to
do so in that gem of a small theater, the Redoutensaal, in the
Hofburg Palace. "Theater" is a poor word because it con-
notes to us a proscenium arch, boxes, galleries, and so on.
This beautiful and simple eighteenth-century hall has none
of these. It is all one rectangular room. The seats, with
capacity for about one hundred and fifty people on either
side of a central aisle, slope to a shallow orchestra pit. The
stage is behind this at about the head-level of those in the
front row. No part of it is hidden from any seat. The
scenery is permanent, a graceful double staircase at the back
of the stage meeting before a doorway. Side entrances are
also doors. Indoor or outdoor effects are given by screens or
trellises skillfully placed. No setting could have been more
in harmony with Mozart's music.

It is a hard theater, I was told, for singers trained for La
Scala, Covent Garden, the Vienna State Opera House, or the
Metropolitan. In such an intimate place the full power of
their voices would be overwhelming. So intimate is this
lovely room that it carried to us conviction of the truth that
the incomparable performance delighting us was given for a

small group of friends. Without presuming to the role of music critic, we thought both singers and orchestra performed flawlessly, as we told them in expressing our thanks when, on the Chancellor's invitation, during an intermission, they joined us for a glass of champagne in what had been the Emperor's retiring room. Some opera-goers will get an idea of the extent of our pleasure when I add that in the cast that evening were Hilde Güden and Maria Reining.

The next day was devoted to the duties of a state visit. There is no need to describe the calls, receptions, and tours which play so large a part in it. These, in a visit designed to further friendship and good relations, are usually designed to advance the cause. Brevity in a visit is much to be desired. Both visitor and visited, as all of us know, can exhaust the springs of hospitality on one side, and of interest in the unfamiliar—which soon becomes very familiar, indeed—on the other. Again, so it seems to one visitor, a Cook's tour, a dozen countries in as many days, does not pay a unique compliment to each host. The calls become like those of official ladies in Washington twenty-five years ago who used to drive about town all afternoon paying "calls," without moving from their cars, by having a servant leave with whoever opened the door cards with the right-hand upper corners turned down to show that the caller herself was in the vehicle. Cheating was severely punished by a sensitive public opinion. The ritual constituted a call by and upon harassed chatelaines who wanted nothing more than the symbol. Whenever the receiver of the card was so ignorant as to say madame was at home and would be delighted to receive the caller, a foul play had been committed and was deeply resented. It struck at the heart of the system.

In the same way, some state visitors make a great play for popular acclaim, sometimes, so it seems, just to exceed the crowd estimates of an earlier visitor, and sometimes to stir up elements of the local population to the detriment of the host government. Whatever the purpose, these attempts at popular triumphs always present grave problems to the host in protecting its visitor. As an attempt at subversion this sort of thing is justifiably resented. The size of crowds turning out for a visitor is usually misunderstood or exaggerated as an indication of lasting opinion. Curiosity and manipulation can be quite as strong a motive force for mass attendance as approval; and, where the individual does approve, the emotion is quite likely to be a shallow or ephemeral one. Street crowds are fickle. One day they will cheer the United States; the next week, wreck its Embassy and Information Office. The popular good will generated by state visits is a highly perishable commodity.

Deeper and lasting emotions of friendship do exist, but they are apt to be held by those less likely to line the streets. I have on my desk an excellent bronze figure of a bear standing erect. It was given to me after a press conference in Vienna by an American correspondent acting as an intermediary for his landlady. "Please give this to Mr. Acheson," she said to him, "from an old woman as a thank offering for keeping the bear from her door." Her emotion was not ephemeral.

The public aspects of these visits are not unimportant, but lie less in some abstraction called "good will," than in gaining support for policies upon which the two governments have found, or are seeking, agreement. Here, again, we must be careful. A third maxim, so it seems to one more visited than visitor, is that a state visit should not be used to get something. Too often official visitors have urged a grant, loan, military equipment, or a political undertaking under the not too gentle blackmail that for them to go home "with empty hands," would be harmful to them as well as to us. I have felt my heart turn to ice under this treatment.

During our visit to Vienna our engagements and routes were made public so that those who wished could see and greet their visitor. My desire was to show appreciation of the crushing popular response against those who attempted to organize protests against this visit, as well as disorder and riots. Communist posters had been torn down and defaced, meetings organized to protest had been invaded and taken over, with the result that not one instance of discourtesy or disorder occurred. On the contrary, people would turn out of shops or houses in a wholly unorganized way to wave handkerchiefs, doff hats, and call out some greeting.

Our morning calls at the Austrian Chancellery accomplished another purpose of a state visit of special importance where distance limits opportunities for personal talks. With Ambassador Donnelly to guide us we talked over with the Chancellor, Vice Chancellor, and other Ministers an accumulation of matters to which cable correspondence had not brought solutions, in many cases because one side or the other had not understood an unfamiliar local situation far away. We talked, too, about the central preoccupation of the peace treaty. How could the Russians be induced to move? It was useful and important to explore every avenue with our hosts, even though they all led to the same impasse. It fortified their belief that we were as eager as they were to end the occupation and make Austria once more a free and independent state.

The most moving of my calls that morning was upon the President of Austria, a noble old gentleman, General Koerner. A veteran of the First World War, indeed, a general at that time, he had now been drafted to be the symbol of national unity. A small, slim man, very erect, balding, with almost florid cheeks, bright blue eyes, and a square white beard, he strongly recalled Bernard Shaw, but a very dignified and slightly sad Shaw. The President received us in that portion of the imperial apartments, lost in the vast complex of the Hofburg Palace, which was his official residence. One felt that he must be very much alone with his memories in those large, ornate, and cheerless rooms. He told us that, years ago, as a young officer, he had served His Majesty, the Emperor Franz Josef, in this palace. Then the Austro-Hungarian Empire was one of the great powers. At the end of the First World War Austria was stripped of its empire and became a barely viable republic, and a socialist one at that. But the old General had served his country as best he could. Then came Hitler and another war; and now this. "This" I took to mean an occupied country dependent on the will of others; and, also, the old General, a remnant of the past alone with ghosts in these silent rooms.

"Vienna," he said, "is an imperial city without an empire. Come, I will show you." He led us through room after room, stopping to show us a clock, a masterpiece of its time, which had been a wedding present to Maria Theresa. When the hour struck, the most complicated maneuver had once taken place, in the course of which, as I remember it, a heavenly host descended to crown Maria Theresa and her bridgegroom with celestial garlands. But the clock was not going.

On we went until we came to the balcony on which the Emperor had stood on his birthday to take the salute of his troops massed in the great parade ground below, and the cheers of an endless throng of subjects beyond them. The setting is magnificent and beautiful. Beyond the palace grounds and gardens lies the Ring, a spacious open circle around which are placed grandiose government buildings and the Opera, with famous Gothic churches and the city beyond.

As we gazed in silence over this magnificence and beauty, the old General said, almost as though talking to himself, "Once the lives of fifty million people centered here. Now our poor seven million cannot afford such grandeur." We said our farewells with deep respect and left him once more alone.

All who have visited Vienna will know with what joy we saw its sights and listened to the history with which each of them was encrusted. An experience of this sort always recalls to me an earlier visit in Paris to the Place des Vosges, once the Place Royale, where Henry IV and his court had lived. When we were shown the spot in the street leading up to it where the King had been assassinated, one of the security guards voiced my own sentiments when he exclaimed, "Gosh, Mr. Secretary, there's a hell of a lot of history around here!"

For a few minutes that afternoon in the Schönbrunn Palace the past seemed to be caught and held. The Schönbrunn was the imperial summer palace on the outskirts of Vienna set in spacious gardens beyond which a lawn-covered hill rises for half a mile or more to be crowned by the Gloriette, a series of triumphal arches outlined against the sky. Walking through the palace we came on the schoolroom of Maria Theresa's children. Some of the work of their drawing class had been framed and hung. At a glance it was apparent that one pupil stood out from the rest. I put on my glasses to see who the budding artist might be. The drawings which caught my eye were those of Marie Antoinette. For a moment the room became full of children again. The drawing master was praising the work of a pert and pretty little girl who was taking pre-eminence as her due, while fending off attempts of vengeful brothers and sisters to pinch her and pull her hair. As yet the long shadows had not reached out toward her. The Fates were not yet spinning her life cord from long strands of folly and recklessness, born of willfulness and despair; nor was Atropos ready with her shears beside the guillotine. So much were these thoughts in harmony with the mood I had caught in the Hofburg that I came back with a start to the sunny afternoon and the company of friends.

Melancholy was quite banished from the state dinner that evening, as, indeed, it was from the reception which the Donnellys gave for us in the embassy garden toward the end of the afternoon. Even the Russian High Commissioner, General Sviridov, came to the reception and was affability itself. Two other fellow guests were destined, unknown to any of us, to become our very warm friends. Sir Harold and Lady Caccia—he was then the British High Commissioner— four years later took over the British Embassy in Washington. Happily they are still (1961) in residence.

State dinners by and large are difficult events into which to infuse an atmosphere of relaxation, to say nothing of gaiety. The guest list is severely limited by protocol; and the seating, if one is wise, is wholly prescribed by it. Here form and rank alone can protect one against such fury born of outraged vanity as can wreak untold damage. Let no one look upon a *Chef de Protocol* with condescension. So the dinners are apt to be stiff as the diners explore with hitherto unknown neighbors the possibilities of language and interests.

One can sometimes get caught out by overconfidence. At a dinner my wife and I gave for President Dutra of Brazil, an old soldier and as silent as they are supposed to be and rarely are, the seating arrangement required, for a reason I now forget, that General Dutra should be on my right with my wife on the General's right. We both talked with him, getting monosyllabic answers, until all the parties needed a brief rest. As I looked about, a question leaped to my mind needing an immediate answer. Since the General seemed absorbed in his dinner, I said quietly across him to my wife, "Who is that striking blonde halfway down the table on your right?" Without benefit of translation of my question, the General said to my wife through the interpreter, "Does your husband often ask you such interesting questions? I must confess that this one had occurred to me, too."

Our state dinner in Vienna surmounted these obstacles in a series of giant leaps. To begin with, it was held in one of the loveliest rooms in the world, the room in the Ballhausplatz, where the Congress of Vienna met, a room of perfect proportions and décor, of exquisite crystal chandeliers in which hundreds of candles twinkled. The story is that two doors had to be added to its original three so that at the Congress five monarchs could enter simultaneously and none yield to another. The U-shaped table was set with historic silver and porcelain, flowers were everywhere, and a symphony orchestra played for us. Interpreters were strategically placed to give aid where it was needed; and, need I add, in Austria, particularly in Vienna, the gift of entertaining talk comes with speech.

As I drank in the sparkling beauty of that room I thought for the third time that day, *"Sic transit gloria mundi."* In geologic time it was only a moment ago that other figures filled this room—the Prince of Benevento, M. de Talleyrand himself, limping from group to group, raising France like a phoenix from the ashes of Napoleon's consuming ambition; Lord Castlereagh, handsome, charming, wise, waiting restlessly for the meeting to end so that he and the wife to whom he remained the lover could hurry off to their dancing lesson, the black despair which in the end drove him to take his life then only a shadow passing almost as it came; Metternich, silent, watchful, a product of the same school as Talleyrand; the Czar Alexander I, talking liberalism and acting the autocrat. How one longed to work the celestial mechanism of time so that they could be with us for the evening. What would we talk about? I asked Justice Holmes this question when, one afternoon, he commented on the difference in our ages and said he had spoken to Lincoln and had talked with a man who had talked with Washington. He went on to add that men similarly spaced in age, until the oldest would have lived before recorded history, could all be brought together in his drawing room. "But could they talk together," I asked him, "and what would they talk about?"

"They would find a way to talk," he said, "through a series of interpreters; and the talk would be about the one subject they would all have in common—women."

The dinner and wines were excellent; the speeches less so. At length the Chancellor rose and offered his arm to my wife. Not until a year later did I know of the drama enacted at that moment, so smooth was the performance. The skirt of my wife's evening dress was given a crinoline effect by a petticoat designed for that purpose. As she rose something gave way. She knew at once that the situation was both critical and serious. A plea to the Chancellor to pause a moment while she enlisted feminine help produced only a genial smile and a movement forward, as the essential inter-preter had already gotten out of the way of the procession. With a split-second decision worthy of a jet pilot and while still behind the table, she let go of the rapidly sagging gar-ment and gave it a gentle kick under the ample tablecloth. As she led the diners to their coffee and liqueurs, her dress became a fitting replica of that straight Grecian style familiar to us in portraits of Napoleon's Empress, Marie Louise, and in which she doubtless appeared many times in that very room.

Years later one of the guests that evening who had observed this little drama with considerable amusement confessed that soon afterward she got her comeuppance through the same experience in the same room.

The Chancellor had told us that after coffee we should have a surprise; and a most delightful one it was. In the ballroom of this great building the little girls of the Vienna ballet school danced for us. They were mere children, the oldest in their early teens and the youngest six or seven. The grace and skill of the older girls, their mastery of the serene composure of the *corps de ballet,* which makes their dancing appear so effortless, was most impressive. The little ones still wore frowns of concentration, were delightfully wobbly, but no one took a spill although there were a couple of close calls. In the last ballet each child carried a small bouquet backed with lace paper. With the last note they ran toward their audience and with a deep and sometimes unsteady curtsy presented each lady with a bouquet.

That evening lives brightly in many memories. As at last we and the Donnellys got into the car to go home, the *Chef de Protocol* murmured to my wife, "Madame's article is in the trunk."

"Did you leave something?" I asked rather unnecessarily.

"Yes," she said, "my fur. It was too warm for it." The ladies did not even smile.

By ten the next morning, after many affectionate farewells and loaded with gifts and flowers, and now shrunk to a little group of four with our faithful friends and aides Barbara Evans and Luke Battle, we were airborne in the *Independence.* Colonel Williams set her course to cross the Alps, pass over the Pillars of Hercules, and skirt the coast of Africa to Dakar. The next day would take us across the Equator and the South Atlantic.

AFTERWORD

A retributive justice requires one who has written a book to read it many times before its debut. This can bring hallucinations. I wrote this book to give myself the pleasure of reliving experiences with some remarkable men, and with the hope that others might know them better. Rereading it, I wonder whether it does something more—not much more, but a little.

Discussing the "old diplomacy," introduced by Richelieu, which was the principal diplomatic method until the First World War, Sir Harold Nicolson wrote that a main characteristic "was the rule that sound negotiation must be continuous and confidential. It was a principle essentially different from that governing the itinerant public conferences with which we have become familiar since 1919." And he quoted François de Callières, a practitioner of this school, to the effect that "open dealing is the basis of confidence. . . . The negotiator therefore must be a man of probity and one who loves truth; otherwise he will fail to inspire confidence. . . . The secret of negotiation is to harmonize the real interests of the parties concerned. . . . Menaces always do harm to negotiation." In short, his conclusion is that "sound diplomacy is based on the creation of confidence and that confidence can be inspired only by good faith."*

We are all familiar with Molière's character who had been

* Harold Nicolson, *The Evolution of Diplomatic Method* (Constable & Co., Ltd., London, 1954), pp. 75, 63–64, 62.

199

speaking prose for forty years without knowing it. Is it possible that the men of whom I have written here, and some
others, such as Alcide de Gasperi of Italy, practiced without
knowing it the best diplomatic method which has yet been
devised? Is it possible, too, that confidence inspired by good
faith and open dealing—perhaps by affection also—gave them,
for even a brief time, the power to influence the course of
events? The confidence, I submit, did exist. The extent of its
influence is for others, coming later, to assess. But I venture
the belief that it played a useful part; and I venture to ask
a question. Today great emphasis is laid upon what is called
projecting an image of ourselves upon the minds of other
men. Doubtless this is most important. But are not the au-
thenticity of the image and its character important, too? And
do not both lie more in the realm of what we do than in the
technique of projection? The Marshall Plan for instance, projected, by the mere doing of it, an image of America of which
we can be forever proud. It was the soundest diplomacy because it created confidence inspired by good faith—and by
good works.

INDEX

Abdul Hamid, 184
Acheson, Mrs. Dean, 8, 10, 12, 19–20, 34, 59, 62–63, 71, 90–91, 107, 110–111, 178–179, 195, 197–198
Adams, John, 107
Adenauer, Konrad, 31–32, 47, 49, 51, 52, 70, 167 ff., 181–182
Alcibiades, 80
Alexander I of Russia, 196
Alexander the Great, 77
Alphand, Hervé, 33, 42, 43
"American Gothic," 10
American Memorial Library, 185–186
Archimedes, 81–82
Aristotle, 77
arms control, 100–101
Atlantic Command, 65–69
Auriol, Vincent, 53
Auriol, Mme., 53
Austin, Warren, 132
Austria, 181 ff.
Avenida da Liberdade, 109

balanced collective forces, 41
Ball, Joseph, 132
Ballhausplatz, 196
Barclay, Roddie, 20, 21
Barkley, Alben W., 132, 140–141
Battle, Luke, 71–72, 73, 120–121, 198
Beaulieu, Fräulein von, 184
Bech, Joseph, 42, 46
Bevan, Aneurin, 17–18
Bevin, Ernest
    and Atlantic community, 118
    and Bevan, 18
    biographical notes on, 3–5, 19–21, 24–25, 28–29
    and Byrnes, 1
    and Conference of Foreign Ministers, 7 ff.

Bevin, Ernest (cont.)
    and Cripps, 16, 17–18
    description of, 1, 2–3, 32
    in Foreign Office, 16 ff.
    and German steel, 21 ff.
    and Marshall, 1, 2
    and martini, 41
    religion of, 23–24
    and Schuman, 2, 31, 34, 35, 39–40
    at South Pacific, 19–20
    and unified command, 25–27
    and unions, 4–5
    and Vyshinsky, 15–16
Bevin, Mrs. Ernest (Florence "Flo"), 8, 10, 11–12, 20
Bidault, Georges, 48
Biffle, Leslie, 132, 142
Bohlen, Charles "Chip," 87–88, 89
Bonn meetings, 51–53
Borgia, Cesare, 87
Bowley, Prof., 5
Bradley, Omar, 41, 67, 68, 76, 77, 111–112, 163
Brandeis, Louis D., 156
Bretton Woods Agreement, 137–139
Bridges, Styles, 131
Bruce, David, 35–36, 37, 43, 87, 176
Bruce, Mrs. David, 8, 10
Bukharin trial, 87–88
Bullock, Alan, 3 n., 4
Bülow, Prince von, 184
Burns, James H., 162
Byrnes, James F., 1, 85, 87, 149, 150, 153

Caccia, Harold, 195
Caccia, Mrs. Harold, 195
Caesar, Julius, 77, 159
Calhoun, John C., 130, 146
Callières, François de, 199

Carmona, General, 114
Castellane, Boni de, 7
Castelo de São Jorge, 118
Castlereagh, Lord, 196
Cavell, Edith, 32
Cherwell, Lord, 64–65
Chicherin, *see* Ornatsky
China Tangle, The, 149
Christian Democratic Union, 169
Chuikov, General, 89–90
Churchill, Sarah, 62
Churchill, Winston Spencer
  appraisal of, 80–81
  and Atlantic Command, 65–69
  and Bevin, 4
  biographical notes on, 79–80, 81–83
  and champagne, 64–65, 76
  and Eden, 63–64, 82
  and Elizabeth II, 70
  and George VI, 69–70
  on hindsight, 158–159
  as historian, 163–164, 179
  and Hopkins, 61
  and Korea, 72–75
  and Lovett, 76–77
  and Marshall Plan, 163
  and "military mind," 163–164
  and Mrs. Acheson, 62–63
  and NATO, 65–69
  and opposition, 115
  and Roosevelt, 61, 64, 65–69, 78
  as speaker, 155
  and Truman, 75–78
  at White House, 61–62
Churchill, Mrs. Winston, 64, 83–84
Clay, Henry, 130
Clay, Lucius D., 173, 174–175
Clayton, Will, 136
Clemenceau, Georges, 54
Cleon, 80
Cohn, Roy, 54
Coleraine, Lord, 99
Collis, Maurice, 103
Committee of Eight, 123, 124
Committee on Foreign Relations, 142
Common Market, 44
Conference of Foreign Ministers, 1,
  6 ff., 85, 87, 181
Conference on Food and Agriculture,
  98–99
Connally, Tom, 125, 140, 142–145
Cook, Thomas, 184
Cotton, Joseph P., 6
Counter-Reformation, 80

Cripps, Stafford, 16, 17–18, 40
Cromwell, Oliver, 77
Cunha, Paulo da, 47

Da Costa, Gomes, 114
Davis, James, 151–152
De Gaulle, Charles, 54, 56
Dewey, Thomas E., 93
"Die Wacht am Rhein," 82
Dill, John, 148
Dockers' Union, 4–5
Donnelly, Walter, 186, 192, 195, 198
Donnelly, Mrs. Walter, 186
Dulles, John Foster, 13–14, 54, 89
Dutra, Enrico G., 195–196

Eden, Anthony
  and Bevin, 3
  and Churchill, 63–64, 82
  dinner of, 31
  and Elizabeth II, 70–71
  as Foreign Minister, 3, 45, 47, 48,
    50, 51, 52, 70–71, 179
  and Schuman, 179
  as speaker, 34
Edinburgh, Duke of, 70–71
Edward VI of England, 82
Eisenhower, Dwight D., 27, 35, 44, 46,
  89, 148, 153
Elizabeth II of England, 70–71
Elliot, William, 67
Euratom, 44
European Defense Community, 42, 44,
  176–177
European Recovery Plan, 128–130
Evans, Barbara, 72, 198

Farewell to America, 136–137
Faure, Edgar, 48
Fechteler, William, 67, 68
Federal Republic of Germany, 167,
  171, 173, 175–177
Feis, Herbert, 149
Figl, Leopold, 185, 187, 188–189, 190
Fisher, Adrian, 134
Fitts, General, 188
Foreign Mud, 103
Foreign Relations Committee, 127
Forrestal, James V., 150
François-Poncet, André, 31
Franklin, Benjamin, 107
Franks, Oliver, 66, 67, 68
Franz Josef of Austria, 193

Gasperi, Alcide de, 112, 200
General Assembly, 25, 99–100, 104–105, 184
Geneva meetings, 104
George, Walter F., 132, 140, 141–142
George III of England, 17
George VI of England, 69–70
German steel production, 21 ff.
Gifford, Ambassador, 71
"God Save the Queen," 82
Gonçalves, Nuno, 116
Gordon, General, 150
Gould, Anna, 7
Greece, 107–108
Gromyko, Andrei, 15
Gruber, Karl, 186
Gruber, Frau Karl, 186
Güden, Hilde, 190
Gutt, Camille, 175

Halifax, Earl of, 3, 62
Halifax, Lady, 62
Halleck, General, 158
Harriman, W. Averell, 35, 45–46, 48, 75, 76, 92–93, 127
Haslip, Joan, 184
Hatch, Carl, 132
Hayden, Carl, 132
Hayter, William, 91, 105, 182
Henry IV of France, 194
Herbert, Victor, 7
Heuss, Theodor, 167
Hill, Lister, 132
Hilldring, John, 151, 152
Hofburg Palace, 189, 193
Hoffman, Paul, 19, 130
Holmes, Oliver Wendell, 81, 121, 143, 147–148, 196, 197
Hoover, Herbert, 6
Hopkins, Harry, 61, 125
Hughes, Charles Evans, 94
Hull, Cordell, 86, 99, 123, 125–126
Hull, John E., 150
Humphrey, George, 21
Hurley, Patrick, 149

Independence, 16, 119, 121, 185
International Bank, 18, 22, 137, 138, 139
International Monetary Conference, 137–139
International Monetary Fund, 18, 137, 138, 139

Japanese Peace Treaty, 53
Jay, John, 107

Jefferson, Thomas, 107
Jessup, Philip, 20, 89
Jessup, Mrs. Philip, 20
Johnson, Andrew, 33
Jones, Marvin, 98
Joseph I of Portugal, 109

Kennedy, John F., 35
Keynes, Maynard, 139
Keynes, Mrs. Maynard, 139
Khrushchev, Nikita S., 88, 103, 104–105, 183–184, 185
Kirkpatrick, Ivone, 169–170
Kiss Me, Kate, 34
Kitchener, Horatio H., 79
Koerner, Theodore, 192–194
Krug, Julius A., 127
Krutikov, M., 99

La Follette, Robert M., 130, 132
Law, Bonar, 99
Law, Richard, 99
Lehman, Herbert, 125
Lenin, Nikolai, 103
Lie, Miss, 94–95
Lie, Trygve, 91, 93, 94–96
Life and Times of Ernest Bevin, The, 3 n.
Lincoln, Abraham, 33, 82, 115, 140, 197
Lindemann, Prof., 64–65
Lisbon meetings, 47 ff., 107 ff.
Llewellin, John J. "Jay," 96, 97, 98
London meetings, 47, 70, 181
London *News Chronicle,* 39
London *Observer,* 91
Lovett, Robert A., 48, 67, 76–77, 119, 162, 163, 165
Lowe, Robert, 57
Lucas, Scott, 132
Ludlow, Louis, 62

MacArthur, Douglas, 73, 165
McCarthy, Joseph R., 54, 133, 140
McCloy, John J. "Jack"
    and Adenauer, 170, 173, 175–176, 177–178
    appraisal of, 22
    and Bonn meetings, 52
    career of, 22
    and German steel, 22–23
    home of, 51, 167–168
    and unification, 38
McCloy, Mrs. John J., 167–168, 186
McGrigor, Rhoderick Robert, 65–66, 67

McKellar, Kenneth, 134–135, 136
MacVeagh, Lincoln, 107–108, 113, 115, 117, 118, 119
Macey, "Big Ben," 20, 21
Makins, Roger, 76
Mardi Gras, 118
Maria Theresa of Austria, 193, 194
Marie Antoinette, 194
Marie Louise of France, 197
Marriage of Figaro, The, 189
"*Marseillaise,*" 82, 187
Marshall, George C.
    as Ambassador to China, 149 ff.
    biographical notes on, 159–161, 165
    and Davis, 152
    decisions of, 155–158
    description of, 147–148, 159–161
    and EDC, 42–43, 44
    and Marshall Plan, 2, 155, 156, 163
    and "military mind," 163–164
    as raconteur, 160–161
    as Secretary of Defense, 42–43, 161–165
    as Secretary of State, 153–154
    as speaker, 154–155
    and Truman, 147
Marshall, Mrs. George C., 147, 148, 149, 154, 160, 161
Marshall Plan, 2, 19, 35, 56, 104, 127, 128–129, 155, 156, 163, 182, 200
Martin, Mary, 20
"Maryland, My Maryland," 15
Massigli, M., 38, 40
Matthews, H. Freeman, 162
Maybank, Burnet, 132
Melbourne, Lord, 140
Mendès-France, Premier, 54
Menon, Krishna, 102, 103
Metternich, Klemens von, 196
"military mind," 163
Millikin, Eugene D., 131
Molière, 199
Molotov, Vyacheslav, 1, 32, 85, 86
Monnet, Jean, 37, 38, 42, 43, 45–46, 55
Morgenthau, Henry, Jr., 137, 138
Morrison, Herbert, 45, 46
Mozart, Wolfgang, 189
Muhammad Zafrulla Khan, 102
Murphy, Robert, 89
Murville, Maurice Couve de, 33
My Fair Lady, 179

Napier, Lord, 103
Napoleon Bonaparte, 196, 197

Nash, Frank, 119, 120, 121
NATO, 2, 25, 41–42, 46, 51, 65–69, 107 ff., 182
negotiation, 103–105, 199
Nevinson, Henry W., 136
Nicolson, Harold, 199
Nitze, Paul, 72
North Atlantic Treaty Organization, *see* NATO

October Revolution, 85
Ollenhauer, Erich, 171
Ornatsky, George V., 85

"*Painel dos pescadores,*" 116
Palace of Queluz, 111
Palais Rose, 7–10, 88
Palais Rose conference, 88–89
Palais Schaumburg, 178
Palmerston, Lord, 117
Paris meetings, 104–105, 172, 184
Parodi, Alexandre, 33
Patterson, Robert P., 150
Pavlov, M., 86
Pearson, Lester B. "Mike," 5, 65
Pericles, 80
Petsche, M., 40
Philip, Prince of England, 70–71
Pinza, Ezio, 20, 141
Plato, 113
Pleven Plan, 42
Plowden, Edwin, 45–46
Political Committee, 100, 102
Pombal, Marques de, 109
Porter, Cole, 34
Portugal, 108
prisoners of war, 99, 101–103
Prokofiev, Sergei, 90
"public opinion," 55

Quai d'Orsay, 10–11, 15, 32

Raab, Julius, 181
Raphael, Raphaello, 112, 113
Rayburn, Sam, 55
"Red Flag, The," 15
Redoutensaal, 189–190
Reformation, 80
Reining, Maria, 190
Republican Policy Committee, 131
Reston, James B., 145–146
Ribbentrop, Joachim von, 85
Richards, James P., 120
Richelieu, Cardinal, 199
Robbins, Thomas H., Jr., 27

Romano, Giulio, 112
Romeo and Juliet, 91
Roosevelt, Franklin D.
  and Atlantic command, 65–69
  and Churchill, 61, 64, 65–69, 78
  and Conference on Food and Agri-
    culture, 98
  desk of, 115
  and Korea, 73
  and Molotov, 85
  as speaker, 155
  and Vandenberg, 125
Russell, John, 97, 98
Russell, Richard, 132
Russian music, 90–91

Salazar, Antonio de Oliveira, 111, 112,
  113 ff.
Salisbury, Lord, 17
Schaerf, Adolf, 187
Schine, David, 54
Schmid, Carlo, 171
Schönbrunn Palace, 194
Schumacher, Kurt, 171–172
Schuman, Robert
  appraisal of, 54
  and Bevin, 2, 31, 34, 35, 39–40
  biographical notes on, 31–32
  at Bonn, 51–53
  and Conference of Foreign Minis-
    ters, 5–6, 10–11, 14–16, 21, 23 ff.,
    178, 179
  description of, 31, 32, 50
  and EDC, 44 ff.
  and Elizabeth II, 70, 71
  and English language, 33, 34–35
  and German steel, 36–37
  and Lisbon meetings, 47–51
  and NATO, 41–42, 119
  and "public opinion," 55
  and Schuman Plan, 36 ff.
  and unification of Western Europe,
    36 ff., 118
Schuman Plan, 36 ff., 42
Schumann, Maurice, 33
Sergeev, Vasili A., 96–97
Shakespeare, William, 34, 82
Shaw, Lord, 5
Sheba, Queen of, 183
Sherbrooke, Viscount, 57
Shinwell, Emanuel, 27
Shostakovich, Dimitri, 90
Smith, Walter Bedell, 159
Smoot-Hawley Tariff Act, 19
Snyder, John, 18, 48, 119

Social Democratic Party, 171
Socrates, 77
"Some Enchanted Evening," 141
South Pacific, 19–20
Spain, 108
Stalin, Joseph, 2, 87, 105, 114
"Star-Spangled Banner, The," 187
state dinners, 195–198
state visits, 181 ff.
steel production, German, 21 ff.
Stevenson, Adlai, 54
Stikker, Dirk, 46
Stimson, Henry L., 22, 157, 165–166
Strang, William, 2
Sviridov, General, 195
Swan Lake, 91

Taft, Robert A., 54, 130, 131, 133, 140,
  177
Talleyrand, Prince Charles de, 196
Talleyrand-Périgord, Duchesse de, 7
Taming of the Shrew, The, 34–35
Taylor, Maxwell, 89–90
Three Wise Men, 45–46, 48–49
Tobey, Charles W., 137–140
Tocqueville, Alexis de, 141
Trade Agreements Act, 19
Trades Union Congress, 4
trade unions, 3–5, 95–96
Transport and General Workers'
  Union, 4
Truman, Harry S
  and Award of Merit, 161
  and Barkley, 140
  and Bruce, 35
  as bush Baptist, 23–24
  and Churchill, 75–78
  desk of, 115
  and Dewey, 93
  and EDC, 48, 51–52, 177
  and George VI, 69
  and initial S, 144
  and Lisbon meetings, 119, 120
McKellar and, 134–136
  and Marshall, 147, 149, 150, 153
  and Marshall Plan, 128, 129–130
  and re-election, 51, 53
  and Tobey, 138
  and unification, 37, 38
  and Vandenberg, 128, 129–130
Tschaikovsky, Pëtr Ilich, 91

unification of Western Europe, 25–27,
  36 ff.

unions, *see* trade unions
United Nations General Assembly,
  see General Assembly
UNRRA, 124–127

Vandenberg, Arthur H.
  appraisal of, 130–131
  and Committee of Eight, 123–124
  and Connally, 142–145
  "conversion" of, 124
  and ERP, 130
  and Foreign Relations Committee,
   127
  and Hull, 123
  and Marshall Plan, 128–129
  and Taft, 131
  and UNRRA, 124–127
  and Vandenberg Amendment, 128
Vienna, 181 ff.
Villa Madama, 112

Vinson, Fred M., 141, 144
Voltaire, François, 77
Vyshinsky, Andrei, 12, 14, 15–16, 87 ff.

Wagner, Robert F., 132, 137–138
Washington, George, 77, 197
Webster, Daniel, 130, 146
Wherry, Kenneth S., 131, 133–135
White, Wallace, 132
Wilhelm II of Germany, 184–185
Williams, Francis, 119, 120–121, 198
Williamsburg, 64
Wood, Grant, 10
Woodward, Stanley, 87
Wright, Jerauld, 46

Xanthaky, Ted, 115, 118

Yale Corporation, 133
Young, G. M., 44

ABOUT THE AUTHOR

DEAN ACHESON, born in Middletown, Connecticut, graduated from Yale and the Harvard Law School. He was law clerk to Associate Justice Louis D. Brandeis for two years, after which he joined a law firm in Washington, D.C.

In 1933 Mr. Acheson served as Under Secretary of the Treasury for six months. In 1941 he was appointed Assistant Secretary of State, served as Under Secretary of State from 1945 to 1947, and was the Secretary of State under President Truman from 1949 to 1953. Having participated in the founding of NATO, Mr. Acheson was asked in 1961 to head an advisory group to work with Secretary of State Dean Rusk in strengthening NATO.

Since 1953 Mr. Acheson has been in private law practice in Washington, D.C. He has written several short stories for magazines, and his previous books are *A Democrat Looks at His Party*, *A Citizen Looks at Congress*, and *Power and Diplomacy*.